THE ENERGY WITHIN: PARISH PASTORAL COUNCILS TODAY

THE ENERGY WITHIN
PARISH PASTORAL COUNCILS TODAY
Discern, Decide, Implement, Involve

Johnny Doherty, Paddi Coyle,
Tony Crilly and Oliver Crilly

VERITAS

Published 2016 by Veritas Publications
7–8 Lower Abbey Street, Dublin 1, Ireland
publications@veritas.ie
www.veritas.ie

ISBN 978 1 84730 765 1

10 9 8 7 6 5 4 3 2 1

Typeset by Padraig McCormack, Veritas
Printed in the Republic of Ireland by SPRINT-print Ltd, Dublin

Cover art work: 'Pentecost' by Colette Clarke is based on an original icon
from Stavronikita Monastery in Mount Athos, Greece and is reproduced
with kind permission of the artist.

Veritas books are printed on paper made from the wood pulp of managed forests. For every tree felled, at least one tree is planted, thereby
renewing natural resources.

Contents

PART FOUR: A STRATEGIC VIEW

The Parish Community

The story of parish pastoral councils is a fascinating story. It is a story of paradox and sometimes of misunderstanding, but most of all it is the story of one of the most significant developments in the Catholic Church in the last one hundred years. It is a development which flows from the insights of the Second Vatican Council. Vatican II gathered the truths and traditions of the Catholic faith and articulated them for our time. Among the insights rediscovered and re-emphasised by the Vatican Council was the vital role of the laity in the life of the Church. The role of the laity cannot be left simply as a nice idea: it has to be incorporated into the structures and activities of the Church's daily life. It is in this context that parish pastoral councils evolved after the Vatican Council, and were incorporated into the new Code of Canon Law in 1983.

The Parish Matters

In Act Three of Brian Friel's *Translations*, Lieutenant Yolland of the British Ordnance Survey has disappeared in suspicious circumstances. Captain Lancey, the senior British officer, bursts into the local hedge school, threatening vengeance. Owen, the son of the hedge school master, is acting as translator for the British officer. Lancey rages: 'If the lieutenant hasn't been found, we will proceed until a complete clearance is made of this entire section'. Owen translates: 'If Yolland hasn't been got by then, they will ravish the whole parish'. Lancey sees the area as an administrative unit, a section on a map. Owen, speaking to his own Irish-speaking community, knows that section means nothing to them, but when he translates it as 'parish', he knows they will understand it as the people of the parish, that they themselves and their neighbours will be at risk. In some Gaeltacht areas even today **pobal** (people, community) and **parish** are practically interchangeable terms.

If you look for 'parish' in Wikipedia, or in the Oxford or Cambridge dictionaries, the first reference will be to 'a church territorial unit', or 'a small administrative district (in the Christian Church)'. However, if you go to the Catholic Church's Code of Canon Law (1983), you will find that the first definition is: 'a certain community of Christ's faithful stably established within a particular Church' (Canon 515). The Code of Canon Law, like the hedge schoolmaster's son, thinks first of the people.

For most Catholics the local parish community is their first experience of Church. We might think that for this reason the role of the parish would be self-evident. But recent challenges, and initiatives aimed at resolving them, have blurred the thinking around parish. The reduction in the number of priests has meant that strategic thinking has been driven by the question of spreading available priests over a broader area, rather than by the challenge of renewing the parish community from within. Similarly, the creation of parish clusters or pastoral areas may have the unintended consequence of taking the focus off the parishes which are grouped in the new wider catchment. This is not to say that these initiatives are not useful or necessary, but it means that when parishes are grouped together in one way or another, attention needs to be focused on the individual parishes and their history and identity, as well as on the newer grouping.

The parish matters. It has mattered in the past, and it still matters today no matter what changes have taken place in the context in which it exists. The more we believe the parish matters, the more we have to take it seriously. We cannot take its role for granted, or leave its progress to chance. We have to work consciously at the building and development of the parish faith community.

> The parish is, without doubt, the most important locus in which the Christian community is formed. This community is called to be a fraternal and welcoming family, where Christians become aware of being the people of God. In the parish, all human differences melt away and are absorbed into the universality of the Church. The parish is also the usual place in which the faith is born and in which it grows. It constitutes, therefore, a very adequate community space for the realisation of the ministry of the Word, at once as teaching, education and life experience.
>
> Today, the parish is undergoing profound transformation in many countries. Social changes are having repercussions on the parish, especially in big cities 'shaken by the phenomenon of urbanisation'. Despite this, 'the parish is still a major point of reference for the Christian people, even for the non-practising'. (*General Directory for Catechesis*, paragraph 257)

The Parish Pastoral Council Matters

It is because we believe that the parish matters that we believe in the vital role of the parish pastoral council. The parish pastoral council is about the parish, and about the renewal and development of the parish. The parish pastoral council is the way forward, because by definition it involves the priest and the people together in working consciously for building up and stimulating the parish as a community which takes responsibility for its own life and growth. In our work assisting parishes to establish pastoral councils, and after a lot of study and reflection, we are convinced:

1. that parish pastoral councils are at the core of pastoral development and maintaining a vibrant parish life;

2. that how we approach them and what we call them matter enormously;

3. that the reason why these things matter is because parish pastoral councils are not just committees of helpers, but are about co-responsibility and shared leadership in our parishes;

4. that leadership is so fundamentally important that if it is not done properly the results can be destructive.

The way of life of the parish pastoral council, including the priest, is about discerning the pastoral needs and potential of the parish, reaching decisions by prayerful consensus, implementing the decisions, and involving the people of the parish in taking responsibility for the life of the parish. Discerning is not about looking at the needs of the members of the parish pastoral council, or the needs of any individual or group in the parish. It is about finding what this parish community needs, now and into the future.

The parish pastoral council is unique in its role. It is at the heart of the parish, and at the heart of policy-making and strategic planning for the parish. It lives and works among real people and real issues. For this reason, the process of discernment, decision-making, implementation and involving others has to be located in the concrete reality of parish life, of parishioners' lives. Different priorities may surface at different times. We propose a framework of six ongoing priority areas, based on the documents of Vatican II and on the priorities which surfaced in the parish surveys and at the parish assemblies during the pastoral councils' development process.

These six priorities are:

1. The empowerment of the laity for leadership;

2. Being and building a community of faith in the parish;

3. Marriage and family life: the Domestic Church;

4. Children and young people: handing on the faith;

5. Ecumenism: building bridges with other Christian Churches, alienated Catholics, people of other religions, and people of no faith;

6. The social teaching of the Church: our mission in and to the world.

The Holy Spirit Matters

It is our conviction that if one thing more than any other is necessary for the successful development of a parish pastoral council, it is faith in the presence and power of the Holy Spirit. The structures and processes we devise for the involvement of the laity and for collaborative leadership in our parishes need to be processes which facilitate discernment and consensus, processes which are open to the guidance of the Holy Spirit.

Being guided by the Holy Spirit is not about having a vague pious aura. The Holy Spirit is a spirit of unity and unselfish love, a spirit of reconciliation and encouragement. The Holy Spirit will not guide us into decisions or actions which are self-serving or motivated by sectional interest. On the other hand, the Holy Spirit will give us the courage and integrity to do difficult things because they are right.

The successful development of a parish pastoral council is a priority because the parish is still where the future of the local Church is determined. It is still the pre-eminent place for catechesis, for pastoral development and for the new evangelisation. Building a vibrant faith community is at the heart of sharing the Good News. That's what really matters.

Feast of Our Mother of Perpetual Help,
27 June 2016

PART ONE

Building Partnership

Flowing from their rebirth in Christ,
there is a genuine equality
of dignity and action among all of Christ's faithful.
Because of this equality they all contribute,
each according to his or her own condition and
office,
to the building up of the Body of Christ.

The Code of Canon Law,
Part One: Christ's Faithful,
Canon 208

The Church Led by the Spirit

On Thursday 11 October 1962, after a night of heavy rain, Pope John XXIII celebrated Mass in his chapel in the Vatican about 6.30am. He was calm and prayerful, but it was a day of excitement. On this day he was to open the Second Vatican Council.

John XXIII was already an old man, in failing health. He was elected as a stop-gap Pope, expected merely to keep the wheels gently turning until a more energetic successor would take over. And yet, within months he had called the Second Vatican Council and mobilised the worldwide preparation for the most extraordinary event in the life of the Catholic Church in the twentieth century. The agenda for the Church for the foreseeable future was about to be set.

Humanly speaking, it made little sense, yet the aging Pope, struggling with illness, set free the Holy Spirit to blow through the Church and to bring about remarkable change.

The agenda developed during the Council is still accessible through the official documents of Vatican II. However, it is not just the final words of the documents which communicate the direction set by Vatican II. The whole process of the Council showed how the Spirit works in the Church through the gathering of Pope, bishops, priests and laity in serious reflection and prayer.

Wherever we are, if we want to discover the Holy Spirit's agenda for us in the Church in our particular place and time, we should draw on the same resources that Pope John XXIII drew on. He gathered the Church from the four corners of the world; he listened to the consensus which developed, led by faith and prayer and honest dialogue, and before the Council had completed its task, he bowed out: 'Unless a grain of wheat falls on the ground and dies, it remains only a single grain; but if it dies, it yields a rich harvest' (Jn 12:24).

Finding the agenda in our parish setting is not a theoretical task. It involves gathering people together in openness, praying together, listening to one another and to the word of the Scriptures, learning to be disciples. It means trusting in God's Spirit and learning to be surprised, for the agenda of the Spirit is not to be confined within our limited expectations. Pope John XXIII, speaking to one of the many groups whom he received in Rome, described his first inspiration for the Vatican Council as 'a grace of intense perception of the Lord, as the two disciples on the road to Emmaus, with the same notes of surprise, stupefaction, commotion. It came out like a humble wild flower hidden in a meadow: you hardly see it, but you sense its perfume'. (cf. Reflection of Fr Loris F. Capovilla, Secretary to Pope John, in *Vatican II By Those Who Were There*, Chapman, 1986.)

Pope John XXIII had an extraordinary sense of God's guidance, certainly in the Word of God in the Scriptures, certainly in the teaching and tradition of the Church, but also in a calm and fearless appreciation of God's presence in the world in which we live: in its needs and challenges, in every human situation, and in the signs of the times. Pope Francis canonised Saint John XXIII in 2014.

In a letter at the turn of the century Pope John Paul II called on local churches across the world to move, 'to put out into the deep'. His image suggests powerfully that we leave the safe confines of the harbour of routine pastoral practice in a commitment to bringing the Gospel to the people of the twenty-first century. This does not involve an essentially new programme for the Church. The Gospel message is the same as ever. 'It has its centre in Christ himself, who is to be known, loved and imitated.' But the changing circumstances require that the pastoral methods we use be adapted to the circumstances of each community. 'I therefore earnestly exhort the Pastors of the particular churches, with the help of all sectors of God's people, to plan the stages of the journey ahead' (*At the Beginning of the New Millennium*, p. 29). Pope Francis canonised Saint John Paul II in 2014.

When saints are canonised, it is not just a statement about their personal sanctity – it proclaims the witness of their lives as a significant guide to the Church of our time and as a model worthy of imitation. In his homily for the canonisation of Saints John XXIII and John Paul II, Pope Francis highlighted their boldness and their transparency, their openness to the Holy Spirit and their inspiration to the whole Church.

Saint John XXIII wanted to see the power of the Holy Spirit at work in the Church, in a visible and dramatic way that could be compared to a new Pentecost. Saint John Paul II wanted to see a confident Church that would launch out into the deep. Just as the first Pentecost led to an energy for the spread of the Gospel, he wanted to see a 'new evangelisation' which would bring the Gospel to the world of our time. He wanted the world to feel the joy and energy of the Gospel.

One of our key sources for understanding that joy and that energy in the life of the Church is The Acts of the Apostles, the story of the early Church and the early evangelisation. The Acts of the Apostles is part two of St Luke's writings. Part one is the Gospel of St Luke. They are very consciously structured to flow from each other, in a way to mirror each other: the Gospel as the story of Jesus and Acts as the story of the young Church. Luke's Gospel presents Jesus journeying to Jerusalem, to his death on the cross, and it is from Jerusalem, in the narrative of Acts, that the young Church bursts forth after the Resurrection: from Jerusalem to Judea and Samaria and to the ends of the earth.

The fulcrum on which the twin books of Luke's Gospel and Acts turn is the Day of Pentecost, when the apostles were filled with the Holy Spirit. The Holy Spirit is a central character in Luke's drama – central in the Gospel narrative and central in Acts. In Luke's Gospel we encounter Jesus led by the Spirit, and in the Acts of the Apostles we encounter the Church as a community led by the Spirit. It is of the essence of the Church to be led by the Spirit. Pope Francis writes in *Evangelii Gaudium*, The Joy of the Gospel:

> How I long to find the right words to stir up enthusiasm for a new chapter of evangelisation full of fervour, joy, generosity, courage, boundless love and attraction. Yet I realise that no words of encouragement will be enough unless the fire of the Holy Spirit burns in our hearts. A spirit-filled evangelisation is one guided by the Holy Spirit, for he is the soul of the Church called to proclaim the Gospel.

Pope Benedict XVI and Pope Francis have renewed the vision of their predecessors and their call for the mobilisation of all the people of the Church in the service of the Gospel. At the opening of the Pastoral Convention of the Diocese of Rome in 2009, Pope Benedict said:

> It is necessary to improve pastoral structures in such a way that the co-responsibility of all the members of the

people of God in their entirety is gradually promoted, with respect for vocations and for the respective roles of the consecrated and of lay people. This demands a change in mindset, particularly concerning lay people. They must no longer be viewed as 'collaborators' of the clergy but truly recognised as 'co-responsible' for the Church's being and action, thereby fostering the consolidation of a mature and committed laity. (*Church Membership and Pastoral Co-Responsibility*, 26 May 2009)

Pope Francis advocates a laity that is actively involved in the life of the Church and in the Church's mission:

Lay people are, put simply, the vast majority of the people of God. The minority – ordained ministers – are at their service. There has been a growing awareness of the identity and mission of the laity in the Church. (*Evangelii Gaudium*, 102)

It was Pope John Paul II who made the specific connection between this principle of the involvement of the laity and the development of parish pastoral councils. He quoted from the Second Vatican Council's Decree on the Apostolate of the Laity, and added:

The Council's mention of examining and solving pastoral problems 'by general discussion' ought to find its adequate and structured development through a more convinced, extensive and decided appreciation for 'parish pastoral councils' on which the Synod Fathers have rightly insisted.

Parish pastoral councils are not the only form of lay involvement in the Church, but they are a pivotal structure, and they have been proposed and recommended at the highest policy levels in the Church. In 1983 the new Code of Canon Law included provision for diocesan and parish pastoral councils. The use of the term pastoral council is significant, and indicates a focus on spiritual and pastoral development in parishes, avoiding confusion with administrative and financial matters, which are important but have their own support structures such as the parish finance council.

The Irish Catholic Bishops in recent years have shown their support for the development of parish pastoral councils. In two booklets (most recently *Living Communion*, 2011) they have encouraged parish pastoral councils and have suggested guidelines for their development.

The account of the efforts to implement the policies flowing from Vatican II, papal statements since Vatican II and documents from the Irish Bishops' Conference relating to parish pastoral councils, is a very interesting story. It is a story of steps forward and of hesitations, steps backward and renewed efforts: in other words it is the story of a struggle. We should not be surprised by that. The fact is that the whole process surrounding parish pastoral councils is new. It is new to priests, perhaps even disturbing to some priests. It is new to the people of our parishes. We struggle to adjust to a new mindset. We struggle, in the words of Pope Benedict, 'to renew pastoral structures' and to translate our vision into practice.

That struggle is etched in the history of parish pastoral councils in Ireland since the 1960s and 1970s and right up to the present. In 1971 the Irish Bishops' Council for the Laity produced a booklet called simply *Parish Councils*. It was published that year by Veritas and thousands were distributed to parishes all over Ireland. The demand was so great that a second edition had to be published within the year, and many parishes set about enthusiastically forming 'parish councils'.

But something was missing; there was no clear direction about the role of these new parish councils. There was no definition of the relationships within the parish councils or within the parishes. There was no training for members, and there was no existing model to imitate. Most parish councils, and most priests, grasped at the only models they were familiar with, in business and politics. But these were adversarial models, not suitable for building up a faith community. The sad outcome was that by the time the new Code of Canon Law in 1983 was recommending pastoral councils, many of the new parish councils had ceased to exist or had ceased to function effectively.

It was several years before the effort was renewed, and now it had to cope with the disillusionment caused by the failures of the 1970s. In the mid-1980s the question of lay involvement and collaborative ministry was taken up by the National Conference of Priests of Ireland. It was the main theme for a number of annual conferences, led by invited speakers. One of the most influential speakers was Br Loughlan Sofield. He presented well-researched material on collaborative ministry, and introduced the priest delegates from the various dioceses around the country and from the religious orders to the possibility of developing parish pastoral councils. It was new thinking for a lot of priests, but many brought the idea back to their parishes.

The timeline for rethinking the idea and practice of parish pastoral councils is interesting. The term was used officially in the new Code of Canon Law in 1983. Brother Loughlan Sofield addressed the annual conference of the National Conference of Priests of Ireland in September 1985. In 1987 Columba Press published what was to be a very influential book by Fr Enda Lyons, *Partnership in Parish: A Vision for Parish Life, Mission and Ministry*. The disillusionment following the efforts of the nineteen-seventies began slowly to disperse. But there was no huge national movement. Individual parishes moved at their own pace. The turn of the millennium in the year 2000 gave an energy to pastoral initiatives. Some parishes, like Ardmore in Co Derry, took the opportunity to develop a parish pastoral council. The Ardmore process is described in detail in *Think Big, Act Small: Working at Collaborative Ministry through Parish Pastoral Councils*.

Then a significant change took place. Diarmuid Martin became Archbishop of Dublin in 2004, after a few months as Coadjutor. His belief in the value of parish pastoral councils was such that he made it clear right away that he expected each parish to have a pastoral council. But the really important change was that he established a process for the formation and training of parish pastoral councils. That process was clearly defined, and it was presented in the book *A Handbook for Parish Councils* (*Dublin Diocesan Guidelines*), by Jane Ferguson, published by Columba Press in 2005. Though produced for Dublin, it instantly provided inspiration and guidance for interested parishes throughout Ireland and beyond.

Pastoral councils were encouraged in the Archdiocese of Armagh also, and in 2010 Veritas published a book by Fr Andrew McNally (who served as Director of Pastoral Renewal and Family Ministry in the Archdiocese), and Debra Snoddy and Jim Campbell. It was called *Parish Pastoral Councils: A Formation Manual*. It aimed at 'forming, enabling and sustaining' a parish pastoral council. Armagh has since developed a diocesan pastoral plan (2015-20): *Share the Joy of the Gospel*. Support for parishes and pastoral areas is coordinated by the Armagh Office of Pastoral Renewal and Family Ministry.

The Diocese of Down and Connor developed an approach based on a diocese-wide listening process. Meetings took place in parishes across the diocese in 2011, and a report – The Living

Church Report – was presented to Bishop Noel Treanor in July 2011. Five key areas emerged from the listening process. The first of these was 'a clear desire for enhanced and increased participation on the part of parishioners'. 'The Living Church Report' said:

> Co-responsibility on the part of laity and priests was clearly called for in all Listening sessions. This echoes Pope Benedict XVI's assertion that the laity must no longer be viewed as collaborators of the clergy, but truly recognised as co-responsible for the Church's being and action, thereby fostering the consolidation of a mature and committed laity.

A diocesan Living Church office was set up to coordinate the implementation of the vision that had emerged, and a diocesan congress was held in September 2013.

Various initiatives along these lines were developed in other dioceses through the country. In some dioceses such as Limerick (described in *Intercom*, July/August 2009) the development of pastoral councils was seen as part of a larger plan including the development of pastoral areas in which parishes were grouped together. Limerick took another major step with its diocesan synod in 2016, referred to by Bishop Brendan Leahy as 'a Camino of hope'. It was prepared for by an eighteen month listening process that connected with over five thousand people across the diocese. The three-day gathering of the actual Synod involved four hundred delegates, three hundred of which were lay. The outcomes set a direction for pastoral planning and development into the future (see www.limerickdiocese.org). All of this has led to a situation where any parish wishing to develop a parish pastoral council, or indeed any diocese working at strategic pastoral planning, has a resource of accumulated experience and reflection to call upon.

We, the authors of this present book, have been involved with parish pastoral councils in various ways and in various places since the 1980s. Our experience encompasses Hexham and Newcastle in the north of England, Tuam, Galway and Clonfert, a study day in Kerry, and in the Derry Diocese originally Melmount, Ardmore and Greenlough, and then working with nineteen other parishes as part of a diocesan programme. Father Johnny Doherty facilitated and led several courses on parish pastoral councils over those years in the Redemptorist Retreat House in Esker, Athenry, Co. Galway.

The initiative in the Derry Diocese began with the Council of Priests, who divided into four working groups to explore the pastoral needs of the diocese. One of the groups looked at planning ahead. After a good deal of work within the Council of Priests, the process was widened to involve a full diocesan priests' conference. Following discussion on reducing numbers of priests and possibilities like clustering of parishes, a consensus emerged that the development of parish pastoral councils would be a valuable first stage in building a diocesan response to these wider pastoral challenges.

Due to our previous experience, we were invited by Bishop Séamus Hegarty, and subsequently Diocesan Administrator Mgr Eamon Martin, to set up a programme for the diocese which would facilitate parishes in setting up parish pastoral councils. This programme would provide initial training and an ongoing support programme for the parish pastoral councils as they discerned the way forward. Over a period of about four years we have worked with twenty-one parishes, including Ardmore and Greenlough. It has been a very affirming experience. We have been very impressed by the quality of people in the parishes in every part of the diocese – by their sincere faith and their commitment. It has been a privilege to work with them and help them to realise their potential.

This book contains an explanation of the philosophy behind the approach we have taken to parish pastoral councils and their development. It contains a detailed presentation of the process used, and the text of the resources we have developed. This wasn't a ready-made process: it grew from the experience of working with many parishes, and was formed by the faith and reflection of those who attended parish assemblies and residential training weekends. Although we as a team led and facilitated assemblies and training weekends, this book is not just about what we have taught – it is much more about what we have learned, and we owe a great debt to all those we have worked with since the 1980s and 1990s.

The lessons of the 1970s underlined the vital necessity of clear thinking and planning for parish pastoral councils, and for the development of structures which would include arrangements for training and ongoing support.

But there always exists the possibility that these new structures could be seen as an end in themselves. In fact, the better the structures, the greater the temptation to think that the job is done. However creative and effective the systems may be for developing and supporting parish pastoral councils, they can never be an end in themselves. They must be at the service of the renewal of the Church, of empowerment of the laity and co-responsibility of laity and clergy, and of a new evangelisation. As Pope Francis has stressed, they must be at the service of the Gospel and of the joy of the Gospel.

In our work with parish pastoral councils, one image has served as a reminder that no structure or system is the end of the road. That image is the beautiful Russian icon of *The Descent of the Holy Spirit on the Apostles*. This icon was one of the four icons used during the Eucharistic Congress in Ireland in 2012.

The Apostles are gathered in a horse-shoe shape. The image, like all icons, is symbolic rather than realistic: it points to spiritual reality, not to physical reality. Peter and Paul sit side by side at the top, where beams radiate over the Apostles. Each Apostle holds a scroll or a book, representing the word of God. At the bottom of the picture, at the open end of the horse-shoe, there is a dark doorway, and standing in the doorway a little crowned figure holding a white cloth on which he is gathering scrolls of the word of God. This figure is Cosmos, representing the world which is hungry for the word of God.

We placed this icon on a table, with a lighted candle, at parish assemblies and at the residential training weekends. First of all it highlighted the role of the Holy Spirit as we gathered in prayerful discernment. Secondly it reminded us that the Holy Spirit descended on the Apostles, not for their comfort, but for the sake of the world which is hungry for the word of God. The descent of the Holy Spirit, as Henri Nouwen says: 'always remains a descent into a world yearning for liberation'. He goes on:

> The Descent of the Holy Spirit, as portrayed by the Russian iconographer at the end of the fifteenth century, shows a new community of faith formed by the Spirit of God who dwells in our hearts and who commissions us to liberate our captive world. The icon brings together prayer and ministry, contemplation and action, quiet growth in the Spirit and mission to our restless world. It proclaims that the community of faith is a safe place to dwell, but also a centre from which a call goes forth to liberate the world. (*Behold the Beauty of the Lord, Praying with Icons* by Henri J. M. Nouwen, published by Ave Maria Press, Notre Dame, Indiana)

A parish pastoral council is a community of faith – a forum which enables us to be open to the presence and power of the

Holy Spirit, not for our own comfort, but for the sake of others, so that in prayer and discernment we may seek the guidance of the Holy Spirit, find the way forward for our parish, and have the courage to reach out and involve others in building up our local Church.

A New Way of Working

When Pope Benedict XVI spoke to the Synod of the Diocese of Rome about involving the laity not just as collaborators of the clergy, but as co-responsible for the life of the Church, he went on to say that that could only happen if new pastoral structures were developed. Otherwise it might remain a pious aspiration. Clearly, at parish and diocesan level, the kind of new pastoral structure which can make the difference is the pastoral council: the diocesan pastoral council and the parish pastoral council.

This is a new way of working in the pastoral life and in the pastoral leadership of the Church. And yet, the term pastoral council, and specifically parish pastoral council, has been around so long now that many people presume that they know what it is about. It's not that simple! The concept is still comparatively new, and it will take time and conscious effort to clarify its meaning and significance. Even people who are involved in a parish pastoral council can betray a lack of understanding of the concept by slipping into the practice of calling it 'the parish council', or 'our committee', showing a lack of clarity about its function and its identity. Others easily talk about 'the priest and the pastoral council', forgetting that the priest is part of the pastoral council. Some priests think they have grasped the idea, and yet can say that they have made it clear to 'the pastoral council' that they are free to make their own decisions. That may sound magnanimous, but it misses the point about the process of decision-making. It is not about exchanging decision-making by the priest alone for decision-making by the laity alone. It is about learning to discern together and share in a collaborative leadership.

A New Form of Leadership

The most important thing about parish pastoral councils is that they are a completely new form of leadership in the Church. We find ourselves, consequently, at the very beginning of our understanding of what they are about; how they work; how they can and should develop. Ultimately they are for the purpose of facilitating every baptised, confirmed and admitted to the Eucharist person to take her or his full part in the life of the parish and in the mission of the parish to the world.

However, a parish pastoral council does not represent the totality of leadership in the parish. It is not the overall governing body of the parish. In fact, it is not about the administration of the parish or about the finances or the maintenance of the parish buildings or properties.

When we met parish representatives initially to explore the possibility of setting up a parish pastoral council, it was important to clarify the role and remit of the pastoral council. We addressed this on a study day – a day of reflection on the role of the pastoral council and the kind of process we could help to facilitate in order to develop a pastoral council in the parish.

We began by asking the parish representatives to reflect on what parish meant to them, by writing down and sharing their responses to this question:

What words, phrases, images does the word parish conjure up for you?

We got people to write down their own thoughts; share with one or two people around them; and then gather all these words/images together. The list was always rich in spirituality and in insight.

Some of the words we frequently heard were:

Faith	Loyalty	Church Building
Prayer	Friendship	Schools
People	Ownership	Collections
Families	Priest	One Body
God	Place of Identity	All Inclusive
Community	Christ	Football Teams
Welcoming	Bishop/Diocese	
Support	Worshipping Together	
Love	History – faith handed on	
Mass/Sacraments	Roots/being at home	

Many more words, phrases and images were used but these give a flavour of people's appreciation of the importance of their own parish in their lives.

The parish is a community – and needs to be built as a community. In many parishes there can be two, three or four or more communities. The task is to build one parish without in any way diminishing the importance of each smaller community for the development of the faith of the people.

Today this is becoming more difficult – and more urgent – as the Church experiences a drastic fall in the numbers of priests. In most places we are seeing the clustering of parishes; the development of pastoral communities or pastoral areas, etc. How we deal with this new reality in the years ahead will be very significant for the survival and certainly for the flourishing of the Church in so many of our parishes. New ways need to be tried, ways that will involve the laity of the Church.

As we looked at words, phrases, and images that the word parish conjured up for people, the words 'bishop' and 'diocese' were missing. That is very significant for us as Catholics. When we said that the word bishop should be included in our thinking about parish almost every group were surprised, some even uncomfortable with it. And yet without including the bishop we lose touch with who the parish is.

In our Catholic understanding the parish is a part of the local Church. Because of that the parish community is accountable to the diocese for its faith development, just as the diocese is an integral part of the universal Church and is accountable to it.

The word 'accountable' is an interesting one, isn't it? A lot of people will immediately think about finances, and that is part of it. We found quite a bit of resistance in people to this. We could say that in many parishes the diocese was not part of people's self-awareness.

However, our accountability to the bishop and the diocese is far bigger than the finances. It's about listening to the questions that the local Church and the universal Church are asking. These questions are much bigger and far more challenging than those we could be asking of ourselves if we are closed in on ourselves as a parish. Accountability also means being open to the teaching of the local Church – the bishop and the diocese – and to the universal Church on the major questions that are confronting us today in our world. We do have a Catholic way of seeing things that we can easily ignore and when we do we reduce our practice of the faith to a number of actions that we are engaged in, even though gladly.

The bishop is also intimately connected to each parish by the fact that he appoints the priest(s) to the parish. This is not merely an administrative act. It is also an important part of his pastoral care for the diocese. This is becoming increasingly difficult as the number of priests diminishes. This very fact calls out from the people of a parish a greater generosity in accepting the priest with all his gifts and shortcomings and being willing to work with him for the good of the whole parish and diocese.

Two Distinct Aspects of a Parish

When a priest is appointed to a parish he receives a two-fold appointment. Firstly he is appointed to the **pastoral care** of all the people. Secondly he is appointed to **administer** the parish. These are two very distinct but related tasks.

When we met with people in the parish assemblies and when we met the newly selected members of the parish pastoral councils we asked them to reflect on the question: **What's involved in the pastoral care of the people of the Parish?**

We gave them time to write down their individual responses to this question; then we gathered together as many of their responses as possible. The following list gives a good flavour of these responses.

What's involved in the pastoral care of the people of the parish?

Celebration of the Eucharist
Weekend and daily

Faith development

Preaching

Sacrament of Baptism

Listening/non-judgemental

Sacrament of Reconciliation

Welcoming everyone

Sacrament of the Sick

Care of the priest

Sacrament of Marriage

Eucharistic ministers

Sacrament of Confirmation

Ministers of the Word

First Holy Communion

Bereavement

Sick/Elderly

Caring for the unemployed

Caring for young people

Caring for the poor

Schools

Dealing with people as they are

Hospitality

Involving others – their gifts

Hospitals

Addictions

Nursing homes

Faith development

Counselling

Emergencies

Parish groups

Confirming people in their faith

Retreats & missions

Child protection

Home visitation

Relationships with other Churches/Faiths

We then did the same exercise with the question: What's involved in the administration of the parish? The next list is a good account of what they came up with.

What's involved in the administration of the parish?

Finance
Upkeep of properties
Churches, halls, houses
Cemeteries etc
Record keeping
Fundraising
People management
Parish personnel
Secretaries, housekeeper
Other staff

Communication with: diocese
State, agencies
Paperwork around: Sacraments
Schools
Births, marriages and deaths
Parish newsletter
Parish groups, social groups
Child safeguarding
Youth Club
Wages
Insurance

The purpose of this exercise was not to establish a definitive list of all that's involved in pastoral care of the people and the administration of the parish. Rather the purpose was to highlight how much is involved in each of them. Both lists can be added to. But the overall impact has to be that there is far too much for any one person or even for a small group of people to do.

We get very clear guidelines from Canon Law on how these challenges need to be dealt with. Firstly it is mandated that every parish should have a finance committee or an administration council. This should be made up of people from the parish who have particular competencies in finance, buildings, property, planning etc. Those appointed work with the priest in making decisions about immediate needs; making plans, both short term and long term, for developments in the physical structures of the parish. Generally these decisions and plans are submitted to the diocesan finance/administration group for approval or otherwise.

Canon Law also indicates that there should be a parish pastoral council in every parish. This is dependent on the wishes and desires of the bishop and his advisors, and the fact now is that practically every bishop wants to see a parish pastoral council in every parish.

What does Pastoral Mean?

When we look at the pastoral needs of any parish today we can easily see that they are enormous. This is because these needs are about people of every age, in every situation of life. The priest is there to oversee the marvellous task of responding to them. But he cannot do it on his own – and he should not try to do it on his own.

Pastoral care of the people of a parish is not only concerned with their pastoral needs. We also have to learn to look at the pastoral potential that everyone has through their particular gifts, both natural and spiritually developed. For example we can look at someone who is housebound as a person in need. And of course this is true. But the other truth is that housebound people very often have a special gift of prayer that can be actively called on for the sake of the parish community. This could involve asking them to pray for those who are sick; or for young people who are struggling; or for young couples in their first year of marriage; or for newly baptised babies and their parents, for example. As we make this call on all those just mentioned, we link people with each other through prayer and a real interest in the well-being of one another.

Parish pastoral councils and parish administration councils are both needed in every parish. They are obviously connected to each other but they also need to be carefully separated so that each knows what they are about. This is particularly important for the development of the parish pastoral council. The temptation of those involved in this will always be to wander into areas of administration. This temptation comes from the experience that buildings can seem more important and immediate than the development of people. Buildings are very important. But they should be left to the parish administration council to plan and sort out. Of course individuals who happen to be members of the parish pastoral council could get involved in other aspects of the parish. This however should not become part of the pastoral council meetings, or be at the expense of their contribution to the pastoral care of the people of the parish.

Lay Involvement

For over fifty years, since the Second Vatican Council, the term 'lay involvement' has been used very regularly and called for very forcefully. Of course the reality of lay involvement has been part of our tradition long before that. Now, though, lay involvement has to be actively promoted if we are to become who we are meant to be: a Christian community.

We often associate this involvement of the laity with the growing shortage of priests. The shortage of priests makes lay involvement more urgent today. But the real reason for lay involvement is Baptism. In Baptism each person is established as a disciple of Christ. This identification is furthered by the Sacrament of Confirmation where the gifts of the Holy Spirit in each person are set free for the service of the Church and the world. And every time we celebrate the Eucharist each one is entrusted with the Word of God, the Forgiveness of God, the Salvation of Christ for the sins of the world, the Body of Christ, and commissioned to bring all of that, and more, to the world of our family, our community, and our society. One of the main purposes of a parish pastoral council is to find the ways of freeing up this power of God that is in God's People for the ordinary everyday life of the community as well as the world in general.

Two Ways of Involvement

People can be involved in two different ways in the life of the parish – either as helpers or as partners.

1. **Helpers:** This kind of involvement is always very necessary.

   a. It means involvement in activities that need to be done, and trying to spread the load as widely as possible. For example at every weekend Mass people are needed to take up the collection and then others are needed to count the collection and bank it during the week. People are needed to keep the church clean and in good shape for upcoming events. Sometimes people are needed to look after the car parking either because of the numbers coming, or for security. There are countless activities like this and people generally are very generous in getting involved.

   b. It also means involvement in activities that need to be done differently. This has resulted in the emergence of Ministers of the Word and Ministers of the Eucharist which have changed the experience of the celebration of the Eucharist from being priest-centred where he did everything to being community-centred where it is more obvious that we all have a part to play. Some parishes are now extending this kind of involvement into ministries of welcome, of hospitality, of music etc.

2. **Partners:** This is a whole new insight into an aspect of the involvement of the laity that leads into what a pastoral council looks like and is for.

a. Involvement as partners means being part of the discernment of pastoral needs and pastoral potential of people along with the priest and the others in the group.

b. It means also being part of the decisions that need to be made so as to keep moving the growth of the community forward.

c. It also means being part of the implementation of the decisions that have been made so that this can be as effective as possible within the parish community.

A parish pastoral council is a group of ten to fifteen people who are selected in some way, by the community and from the community, to work together as partners with the priest or priests of the parish to discern the pastoral needs and potential of the people of the parish; they decide on actions and implement these decisions on an ongoing basis for the development of the active faith-life of the whole parish community.

There is More!

A parish pastoral council that does not involve others has missed the point. Parish pastoral council groups continuously fall into the trap of living as if they have to do everything themselves. Perhaps they are more comfortable there than they are in inviting others to be involved. The parish pastoral council needs to learn to involve others as helpers in activities that they are planning. But they also need to include others as partners in particular projects for the building of the community and the evangelisation of the world.

To involve others in particular projects means to involve them, some as helpers and some as partners. Those who get involved as partners are drawn into discerning the needs and potential of others; they become part of the decisions that need to be made; and they become part of the implementation of these decisions. During this process the group needs to be identifying the people they can ask to be involved with them as helpers and others who would get involved as partners. At every stage this needs to be an important factor.

The ultimate aim of the parish pastoral council is to involve every parishioner in the great call to build a vibrant community of faith where everyone is loved and cared for; where everyone is acknowledged as important for the community and with so much to contribute; and where the parish becomes a sign of hope for the world around it, drawing that world into the peace and joy of Christ.

PART TWO

Getting Started

Journeying through the community of the parish to the heart of the local and universal Church.

Survey Questionnaire

In 2010, on the recommendation of the Council of Priests in the Diocese of Derry and with the approval of the Conference of Priests, Bishop Séamus Hegarty offered the opportunity to every parish in the diocese to develop a parish pastoral council, with the assistance of a diocesan support group. This was in accordance with Canon 536 of the Code of Canon Law. We were invited by the diocese to take on the preparation, training and on-going support of the new parish pastoral councils.

Monsignor Eamon Martin, later to become Archbishop of Armagh, then acted on behalf of Bishop Hegarty. He contacted the priests of the diocese inviting them to get in touch with him to book their parish in for developing a parish pastoral council.

Twelve priests responded fairly quickly. The process was in motion!

The first thing the priests were asked to do was to gather an interim core group of six people, women and men, who would manage the next stages of the process. This core group were not to be the parish pastoral council although some were later selected as such. The remit of this group was to organise everything up to and including the parish assembly.

The first four stages of the preparation were:

1. To organise a survey questionnaire to be filled in by all those who attended Masses on a particular weekend in their parish.

2. To compile the results of this survey questionnaire and gather the results into booklet form. IT help was given to each parish to do this.

3. To have these booklets distributed to every home in the parish.

4. To organise a parish assembly to which every parishioner would be invited. These parish assemblies were held on a Saturday or Sunday afternoon. They lasted five to six hours. The agenda for them was:

   a. to discuss the results of the survey questionnaire, its significance for the parish, and to set priorities for the new parish pastoral council from these results.

   b. to select the first half of the membership of the parish pastoral council.

It was very striking how well the interim core groups did all of this even though it wasn't something any of them had done before, and even though they did not fully understand what it was about. It was a job very well done.

Survey Questionnaire

The real starting point for setting up the parish pastoral council was the parish community. We wanted to listen to the experience of the parishioners in regard to their parish; to let them voice their thoughts and hopes; their disappointments and hurts. There are various ways of doing this listening exercise. We chose the way of a survey questionnaire that would then be followed up with a parish assembly.

Mentor in Newry drew up the survey questionnaire for us. One of their specialities was to draw up questionnaires for small businesses with a view to development. They were very familiar with what is involved in parish life.

Five Sections

They divided the survey questionnaire into five sections which correspond largely to the five sections they used for any survey questionnaire, but they adapted it so that it applied to the parish situation.

Section 1: The people of the parish and their relationships with one another; the various levels of involvement of people with the parish; the support levels that people experience within the parish; and so on.

Section 2: The celebration of the various sacraments, including the Eucharist; times of Masses; arrangements for the various occasions that are important to people at different stages of their lives; the levels of support that people experience at these important times.

Section 3: The people themselves; their willingness to be involved; their perception of communication within the parish; finances; decision-making within the parish.

Section 4: How people would like to see their parish in five years' time. There were many headings in this section that dealt with a desire or otherwise for: a parish pastoral council; a parish that would be supportive of marriage and family life; that would encourage family prayer; that would be open to other Christian Churches; that would be inclusive; that would be caring for everyone.

Section 5: This section was largely to gather information about those who answered the questionnaire in regard to gender; age; practice; belonging; present personal involvement; relationships; hurts; difficulties with the teaching of the Church.

A full copy of this survey is included at the end of this chapter. You can see there the details of the questions asked.

Survey Questionnaire to be Filled in at Weekend Masses

We decided that the best way to deal with this survey was to invite people to fill it in during all the Masses in a parish on a particular weekend. This was flagged up the week-end before the date, just to let everyone know that it was going to happen, so that they could make sure to bring their glasses with them! There was a variety of reasons for doing it this way.

1. The very nature of survey questionnaires is that they should have instant responses to the questions. That generally is how all surveys are conducted and they, in the main, produce very reliable results.

The questions are framed in such a way that the responses are simply **Yes; No; Don't Know** or **Unable to Comment**. Everyone has a right and a responsibility to answer all the questions. Several times there is an opportunity for personal comments to be written.

2. It is liturgically acceptable to do something like this occasionally during the celebration of the Eucharist. This survey questionnaire is filled out after the reading of the Gospel and in place of the Homily. It is facilitated by someone who introduces it and who briefly explains how to go about it. This person should continue to encourage people to keep filling it out in such a way that it doesn't take more than ten to twelve minutes, the usual length of a homily. This facilitator should also encourage people to do it in a prayerful silence as each one makes his/her contribution to the picture of the parish.

3. Each person's responses are honoured. But it is the accumulation of the responses that provides a picture of how the parish sees itself. In this regard the frequency of the **Don't Know** or **Unable to Comment** responses is as important a part of the picture as any other.

4. How about those who were not at Mass in their own parish at that particular weekend? A week to ten days should be given for other responses to come back. People are encouraged to take copies of the survey for family members or friends or neighbours who were not able to be there. Again these should be returned within the week to ten days.

5. How about those who have stopped going to Mass for whatever reason? They could be encouraged by family or

friends to fill one out and return it. Also this is a category of people that the parish pastoral council should get in touch with when it has got itself established. A different kind of survey questionnaire could be developed for them and a method of contacting them could be devised.

6. National survey questionnaires are frequently used to test the patterns of political life, especially coming up to an Election time. These are based on a random questioning of one thousand people and their results are often very accurate. In a parish when this survey is done at weekend Masses the percentage of people questioned is very high. Not everyone necessarily takes part. But the picture that evolves from it can be trusted as a very accurate one of the parish community.

7. Sometimes the anxiety is that parishioners would not do this kind of thing. 'The people here' are different! Our experience is very much the opposite. None of the twenty-one parishes in the Derry Diocese where we have run this process, and none in the various parishes in other parts of Ireland, had any problem. In fact every parish community entered into it with great freedom.

What is Next?

When all the questionnaires have been collected they need to be collated. The results are then produced as a booklet which should be distributed to every home in the parish. Hopefully people will read it and talk to each other about it.

Within a few weeks a parish assembly is called to which everyone is invited. The booklet is one of the major items on the agenda for this assembly, particularly looking at how these results help us to build the future.

The booklet and the results of the parish assembly discussion on priorities coming from it are passed on to the parish pastoral council as one of the major parts of their agenda as they move forward.

A full copy of the survey questionnaire now follows. Sometimes people feel the need to adapt it a bit to their own particular needs. However it is important to stress again that this was the work of professionals, and structured to provide maximum results.

The Life and Future of our Parish of _____ *as a Living Faith Community*

This questionnaire is meant to encourage a process of reflection on the life and future of our parish as a living faith community. Your answers will be carefully considered and will help identify the priorities to be addressed in the future by your parish pastoral council.

1. Relationships and Involvement in the Parish

Please think about each of the following and **circle the phrase** which **best** describes your view:

The quality of relationships between priest(s) and people is …	Very Good	Good	Fair	Poor	Don't Know
Relationships between the people and the schools are …	Very Good	Good	Fair	Poor	Don't Know
The work of parish organisations is …	Very Good	Good	Fair	Poor	Don't Know
Co-operation between parish organisations is …	Very Good	Good	Fair	Poor	Don't Know
Involvement of women in the parish is …	Very Good	Good	Fair	Poor	Don't Know
Involvement of men in the parish is …	Very Good	Good	Fair	Poor	Don't Know
The process of decision making in the parish is …	Very Good	Good	Fair	Poor	Don't Know
Involvement of youth in the parish is …	Very Good	Good	Fair	Poor	Don't Know
The level and range of parish based social activities is …	Very Good	Good	Fair	Poor	Don't Know
Relationships with other Christian Churches locally are …	Very Good	Good	Fair	Poor	Don't Know

Support for families in the parish is ...	Very Good	Good	Fair	Poor	Don't Know
Support for bereaved people is ...	Very Good	Good	Fair	Poor	Don't Know
Support for elderly people is ...	Very Good	Good	Fair	Poor	Don't Know
Support for people with disabilities is ...	Very Good	Good	Fair	Poor	Don't Know
Support for sick people is ...	Very Good	Good	Fair	Poor	Don't Know
Support for marriages in difficulties is ...	Very Good	Good	Fair	Poor	Don't Know
Support for teenagers and young people is ...	Very Good	Good	Fair	Poor	Don't Know
Support for single adults in the parish is ...	Very Good	Good	Fair	Poor	Don't Know
Relationships among parishioners are ...	Very Good	Good	Fair	Poor	Don't Know

2. Sacraments in the Parish

Please consider each of the following and **circle the phrase** which **best** describes your views:

Baptism arrangements and support ...	No change needed	Could be improved	Must be changed	Unable to Comment
First Holy Communion arrangements ...	No change needed	Could be improved	Must be changed	Unable to Comment

Arrangements for Confirmation …	No change needed	Could be improved	Must be changed	Unable to Comment
Support for Marriage preparation …	No change needed	Could be improved	Must be changed	Unable to Comment
Arrangements for Marriage …	No change needed	Could be improved	Must be changed	Unable to Comment
Support for couples after Marriage …	No change needed	Could be improved	Must be changed	Unable to Comment
Arrangements for funerals …	No change needed	Could be improved	Must be changed	Unable to Comment
Arrangements for Sacrament of the Sick …	No change needed	Could be improved	Must be changed	Unable to Comment
Times of weekend Masses …	No change needed	Could be improved	Must be changed	Unable to Comment
Participation by lay people in Masses …	No change needed	Could be improved	Must be changed	Unable to Comment

3. Parish Resources

Please give your view on each statement below by **circling Yes, No** or **Unable to comment.**

I consider the involvement of the laity is an essential part of parish life …	Yes	No	Unable to comment
I would be prepared to become more involved in the work of the parish …	Yes	No	Unable to comment

I am well informed about parish activities, events and news …	Yes	No	Unable to comment
I find the weekly bulletin helpful …	Yes	No	Unable to comment
I contribute regularly to church collections …	Yes	No	Unable to comment
I am eligible for and have entered the Gift Aid scheme …	Yes	No	Unable to comment
I understand how and where my contributions are being used …	Yes	No	Unable to comment

Please use the space below if you have any specific comments about **Parsh Resources**:

_____

_____

_____

_____

_____

_____

_____

4. The Parish in the Future

In five years' time I would like to see: (Please tick ☑ the items you consider important)

1.	An active parish pastoral council	❑
2.	Adult religious education programmes	❑
3.	Supports for marriage and family life	❑
4.	Widespread family prayer	❑
5.	Involvement of youth in the life of the Church	❑
6.	Links with other Christian Churches locally	❑
7.	Greater involvement of people in parish organisations	❑
8.	A vibrant Parish Community which: • Deepens faith • Hands on the faith • Encourages all vocations • Is an inclusive community (Gender, social status, age, etc.) • Is a caring community (local needs and e.g. Third World)	❑ ❑ ❑ ❑ ❑

Add other suggestions:

_____

_____

_____

_____

_____

_____

_____

_____

5. **A Little About You** – please circle each answer which applies to you.

Are you:	Male ❏ Female ❏
Are you a native of this parish?	Yes ❏ No ❏

If you answered **No**, how many years have you lived in the parish?

Your age:	Between 12 ❏ and 18	Between ❏ 19 and 30	
	Between 31 ❏ and 55	Between ❏ 56 and 70	Over 70 ❏

Do you attend weekday Masses?	Never ❏	Often ❏
	Seldom ❏	Every Day ❏
Do you attend Sunday Mass?	Seldom ❏	Often ❏
		Every Week ❏

Do you feel you belong to this parish?	Yes	No
Are you a member of any parish organisation?	Yes	No
Are there any issues which are making it difficult for you to belong as a member of our parish community?	Yes	No

Please circle your answer if any of the following apply to you		
I am in a relationship which is not recognised by the Church	Yes	No
There are some parts of the teachings of the Church with which I am uncomfortable	Yes	No
As a woman, I feel undervalued in the Church	Yes	No
I have experienced hurt in the Church at some time and this has not been healed	Yes	No

Thank you for your participation

This questionnaire has been completed mainly at the weekend Masses _____ If you have completed it at home, please return it to the _____ by _____
_____

Thank you.

Parish Assembly

When the results of the parish survey questionnaire have been analysed and collated, they are published in the form of an A4 booklet, which allows for a clearly legible presentation of figures and comments. This booklet is then delivered to every home in the parish, with a letter of invitation from the parish priest to a parish assembly, giving the date and the venue. It is important that every household receives the invitation. It is equally important that those who accept the invitation be made aware that they must attend for the full duration of the assembly. If people felt they could drop in and out 'to see what's happening', the work of the assembly would be disrupted and progress would be impossible.

The parish assembly requires four to five hours, on a Saturday (11 a.m. – 4 p.m., including a light lunch), or on a Sunday afternoon (2 p.m. – 6 p.m., including a tea break). The process of the assembly is carefully structured. It is not a free-for-all meeting with an open agenda where parishioners raise topics at will. It is structured specifically as a working meeting, with two items on the agenda: first, the parish survey outcomes booklet, and second, the process of selecting the first half of the members of the new parish pastoral council, and a meeting with these and the priest(s), who are *ex officio* members of the parish pastoral council.

Opening

The parish assembly day begins with a welcome, and the facilitating team are introduced. It is pointed out that the day is a continuous process of reflection and discernment, and requires participants to stay for the full day. Each person will find on their seat a name tag, pen and notebook, and a copy of their parish prayer. Extra copies of the parish survey booklet are available for those who may have forgotten to bring them.

The pen and notebook are a vital part of the process. Writing is not something which should deter participants. Experience has shown that it can be helpful in many ways. It can be a stimulus to thought. It certainly helps people to retain thoughts and to prioritise them.

One very important value in the context of an interactive process of analysis and sharing is that it gives each person the time and opportunity to note their own reactions before hearing the opinions of others. If a process begins with one person speaking, an extrovert participant can dominate the discussion. If other people have not already noted their own view, they may end up just responding to the dominant voice, either agreeing or disagreeing.

The same applies to the part of the process which involves selecting people as possible members of the new parish pastoral council. If someone proposes a name, it may be difficult not to acquiesce in that proposal, whereas, if everyone has written down a name or names in advance, each person's view can be given equal weight. We found in the selection process that the humble post-it note provided a handy method to get each person to record the names they wished to put forward. The post-it was not the issue, of course. The issue was ensuring that each person's view was given equal weight, whether they were out-going or quiet and diffident.

Parish Prayer

O Jesus,
help us as the parish of

_____

to make you the centre of our lives.

Through the power of your Holy Spirit,
help us to repent
of the wrongs we have done,
that we may be refreshed in spirit
and renewed in hope.

Through that same Spirit,
help us to be good to one another
and to be faithful to you,
as we live out our vocations:
married, widowed, single, priest, religious –
so that our homes and our parish
may be filled with your presence
and be powerful sources
of your peace.
Amen.

After saying the parish prayer together, the following question is given out:

Why did you personally decide to come here today for the parish assembly?

It seems an innocuous question but in practice has given rise to wonderful answers, from the brief 'Out of curiosity' to some remarkable sharings of faith and commitment. People are asked first to write their own answer, and then to form small groups for sharing, followed by some feedback in the large group.

Background

Hymn: e.g. 'Seek Ye First the Kingdom of God', or 'Spirit of the Living God', followed by an explanation of the significance of the hymn.

There follows a presentation about the background to what is being done as parishes work at developing a parish pastoral council: origins in the Second Vatican Council, the 1983 Code of Canon Law, booklets of the Catholic Bishops' Conference, the local Bishop and the support structures of the diocese.

Getting to Grips with the Parish Survey Outcomes

The facilitating group introduce the parish survey booklet. The participants are divided into five or six groups and part one of the survey booklet is divided between them. They are asked to read closely and carefully the section they have been given. Each person is then to decide what they see as the three most important findings in that section. This has several advantages. Firstly, it means that each section is being read carefully, and a number of people are studying every part of the document.

Secondly, each person is reading their own section very carefully, with concentration, because they have something to look for. They are then asked to discuss their choices within their own group and get a group consensus on the three most important things in their section. They are then asked to write the group's findings on a flip-chart sheet. The groups, in turn, place their sheet on a flip-chart stand and present their findings to the full assembly with some comments or explanations.

This exercise is then repeated for part two of the booklet, the comments section. During both parts of the exercise there has been concentrated reading, thinking and discernment and making judgments, alone and in the group, and setting priorities which will have a value as this material is recorded and handed on to the new parish pastoral council.

Selecting the First Members for the New Parish Pastoral Council

Hymn: 'Give me Joy in my Heart'. Explanation of Hymn.

Introduction: when a parish priest is appointed to a parish, his appointment is twofold – to the pastoral care of the people, and to the administration of the parish. A flipchart sheet is divided in two, with the heading **pastoral care** on one side and the heading **administration** on the other. Parishioners are asked to suggest what things belong under each heading, and these are written up on the flipchart. When there is a substantial list on both sides, the facilitator points out that the parish priest has two choices when confronted with these lists of responsibilities: to do it all himself, which is practically impossible, or to involve others. Involving others is best practice.

If he decides to involve others, he again has two choices: to involve them as helpers or as partners. Involving others as partners is best practice, though helpers will always be needed. A parish pastoral council is a structure of partnership. Partnership with parishioners has already been exercised twice in this process: in taking part in the questionnaire survey, and in this parish assembly. The parish pastoral council which is being formed is a selected group of parishioners whose commission is to continue this partnership in leadership with the priests and to extend it. Participants are asked to reflect on the qualities of partnership in their experience and to share them.

Just as the parish priest has two choices, so now the parish pastoral council has two choices, to do it all themselves or to involve others. Involving others is best practice. And they then have two further choices, to involve others as helpers or as partners. The ultimate aim of this process is to build the parish as a partnership between people and priests in the pastoral care of all the people. A major part of the agenda for this will be the parish survey findings, published in the booklet and prioritised in the work of the parish assembly.

The Selection Process

Participants return to their working groups. They pray together in their own group for a few minutes, asking for the guidance of the Holy Spirit as they prepare for a process of discernment. Post-its are given out, and each person is asked to write one name on each of two post-its: proposing two people from their group that they personally would nominate for membership of the parish pastoral council. Each person folds their two post-its separately and places them in the middle of the table. Then the group prays again for a few minutes, before opening the post-its. The nominations are recorded.

The person with the highest number of nominations is asked if they are willing to accept the nomination. They must be prepared to do the residential training weekend. It is important to have the date for the training weekend set in advance. Only one person from the group is selected at this point.

If there is a tie, and both are willing to accept, it is resolved by drawing lots. Once each group has selected one person, the name is written on a flipchart sheet. This process should result in five or six people being selected. With the priest(s) these will form the first half of the parish pastoral council. Their first task, within a week or two, will be to co-opt the rest of the parish pastoral council, taking account of area balance within the parish, gender balance and age balance.

Meeting with the Selected People along with the Parish Priest

The facilitators sum up and conclude the assembly with a prayer and a blessing. They ask the newly selected members and the priest(s), who are *ex officio* members, to wait behind for a short meeting to go over the details of the next stage, and to share names, addresses and contact details such as phone numbers and email addresses.

Residential Training Weekend

When a parish is setting about developing a parish pastoral council, it is not sufficient to gather a group of people and expect them to begin to function without guidance or a sense of direction. Where this has happened in the past, the results have been disappointing, to say the least. In 1971, many 'parish councils' were set up very quickly without planning, without training, and without an agreed working model. Within a few years, sometimes within a few months, the new parish councils failed, in spite of a lot of good will. Planning and training are essential. There is a lot of truth in the saying: 'to fail to plan is to plan to fail'.

In our work with parish pastoral councils, we have always insisted on a residential training weekend for the new parish pastoral councils, including the parish priest and any other priest in the parish. Here are a few of the advantages of the residential training:

1. It takes the entire parish pastoral council, including the priest, away from distraction and interruption, to a setting where everyone can concentrate on the matter in hand.

2. It creates a situation where people experience working together over an extended period of time, which has a

bonding effect, and helps people to get to know the people they will be working with.

3. It slows people down and makes it possible for them to enter into an interactive process where they can share their faith and listen to others share their faith also.

4. Instead of being an hour or two of study, the weekend can be a spiritual retreat. There is time for a reflective celebration of Mass on the Saturday and the Sunday, and time for prayer and singing. It can be a genuine conversion experience, not in the sense of conversion from bad to good, but in the sense of a sincere deepening of spirituality and sense of vocation.

5. As well as being a spiritual retreat, the extended time allows the weekend also to be a practical workshop, where learning is experiential – adults learn better from working together and talking and listening together. Instead of just learning about a parish pastoral council, participants experience *being* a parish pastoral council. Before the weekend is over they will have experienced running their first meetings.

6. The weekend is also an extended catechesis, not just about the meaning and role of parish pastoral councils, but about the meaning of Church (ecclesiology), and about the truths of the Christian faith (theology). They can better appreciate their own role, not just in the parish structures, but in the life of the Church as a faith community. They take time to deepen their spirituality.

7. One of the most significant arguments for the residential training weekend concerns what these members of new

parish pastoral councils are being prepared for. They are being prepared for leadership. If these were people who were simply expected to be a committee of helpers; if the parish priest were going to exercise the totality of leadership in the parish; or if academically trained experts were going to provide all the leadership skills from outside the parish; then why would you invest time, money and training for pastoral councillors? The fact is that these are people of faith, leaders in their parish community and collaborative leaders with their parish priest.

Leadership is not going to come from somewhere else. Leadership cannot be outsourced, contracted out to any 'professional' group or academic expert. Leadership and responsibility remains rooted in the parish and the diocese. Experts and support groups are very important, but they must be at the service of the leadership in parish and diocese. They cannot replace them. We don't need less training for our parish pastoral councils. We need a lot more. We need priests and people to experience training together.

> In virtue of their Baptism, all the members of the People of God become missionary disciples (cf. Mt 28:19). All the baptised, whatever their position in the Church or their level of instruction in the faith, are agents of evangelisation, and it would be insufficient to envisage a plan of salvation to be carried out by professionals while the rest of the faithful would simply be passive recipients. The new evangelisation calls for personal involvement on the part of each of the baptised. (*Evangelii Gaudium*, 120)

Structure of the Residential Training Weekend

The shape of the weekend training has evolved out of the purpose of the programme – to provide introductory training for newly established parish pastoral councils – and has developed year by year with experience and the input of the parish pastoral councils themselves. As a team presenting and guiding the weekend, we did not want to stand apart from the participants, talking to them like experts who had all the answers. We wanted to walk with them on a journey where we could share our experience and listen to their experience, in a reflective and prayerful atmosphere in which we could all be guided by the Holy Spirit.

The journey of the weekend is a personal journey, and is informed by the personal feelings and gifts of the participants. It is a journey of exploration, seeking knowledge and understanding. Beyond this, it is a journey of faith. The weekend experience does not create faith out of nothing, nor does it approach faith as something introduced from outside. It recognises that the participants are people of faith, and builds on the foundation of genuine faith which is already there. The sharing of that faith is the source of greatest energy during the weekend. That in itself generates great confidence and a sense of vocation and commitment.

The training weekend can be provided for one parish, so that their new parish pastoral council, including the priests, can experience it on their own. However, there are strong arguments for providing the residential weekend training workshop for three or four new parish pastoral councils together. Firstly, there are economic advantages in sharing residential and other costs. But more importantly, there are advantages in the sharing and interaction between parishes during the weekend, which often leads to relationships of networking and mutual encouragement afterwards. This kind of encouragement is already experienced during the weekend, as the presence of other parishes reassures each new parish pastoral council that they are not ploughing a lone furrow, but that what they are engaged in is a broadly based initiative involving the whole diocese.

The Friday Evening: First Steps on the Journey

After the usual welcome and practical instructions, the Friday evening programme consists of two sessions. From the start, people are involved through speaking and sharing their responses, guided by questions which encourage personal sharing, sharing ideas and sharing of faith.

The structure of the sessions is simple, consisting of:

1. Hymn followed by prayer

2. Introduction and questions for sharing

3. Sharing responses

4. Reflection based on a passage from scripture

On Friday evening the scripture passages are introduced as a concluding reflection. Scripture is a significant part of the weekend experience, and as we move to Saturday, scripture passages are given a more dominant role, and are used early in the sessions to introduce important themes.

In the first session on Friday evening there are two sharing questions. The first is: **What are three things you like best about the people of your parish?** This question, coming at the very start of the weekend, headlines that our function is not analysing the problems of our parish, or even analysing the structures of our parish, but is about the people of our parish, beginning by taking a positive, personal, look at them. Saint Ignatius Loyola, writing his *Spiritual Exercises*, was very clearly aware that feelings and emotions played a significant role in personal conversion. Saint Alphonsus Liguori, founder of the Redemptorists, was also very aware of the role of feelings and personal motivation in engaging people during parish missions for repentance and conversion.

The training weekend is a conversion experience for very good people, not conversion from evil to good, but conversion from good to better, in St Ignatius Loyola's memorable phrase which became the motto of the Jesuits, *ad majorem Dei gloriam*: in discerning a course of action, do not do just what is for the glory of God, but what is for the *greater* glory of God.

The second sharing question moves from personal feeling to the process of thinking, which also has to play a significant role during the weekend. The question is simply: **What are three things you would like to be clear about by the end of this weekend that would be helpful for you in relation to your involvement in the parish pastoral council in your parish?**

At this point we highlight two things for the participants: the focus of the weekend and the purpose of the weekend.

Focus of this weekend:

The parish pastoral council in your parish.

Purpose of this weekend:

1. to understand more clearly what a parish pastoral council is and what it is not;

2. to work at how to be a parish pastoral council in your parish;

3. to look at your own personal involvement with, and investment in, the development of your parish through your parish pastoral council.

Scripture Reading: The vine and the branches (Jn 15)

I am the vine,
you are the branches.
Whoever remains in me, with me in her or him,
bears fruit in plenty.

If you remain in me
and my words remain in you,
you may ask what you will
and you shall get it.
It is to the glory of my Father that you should bear much fruit,
and then you will be my disciples.
As the Father has loved me,
so I have loved you.
Remain in my love.
If you keep my commandments
you will remain in my love,
just as I have kept my Father's commandments
and remain in his love.
I have told you this
so that my own joy may be in you
and your joy be complete.
This is my commandment:
love one another,
as I have loved you.

You did not choose me,
no, I chose you;
and I commissioned you
to go out and to bear fruit,
fruit that will last;
and then the Father will give you
anything you ask him in my name.
What I command you
is to love one another.

Reflection

- This reading is about Jesus, and it's about us. We are people of faith.
- We accept the first part of the statement, that Jesus is the vine. We know we need him: our deepest spiritual energy flows from him into us, as the life flows from the tree into every branch.
- The second part of the statement is more difficult for us to accept: You are the branches. We don't see ourselves as that important. And yet, Jesus is saying that he needs us just as much as we need him.
- The fruit doesn't grow directly on the tree. The fruit grows on the branches. Jesus needs us to go out and to bear fruit, fruit that will last.

During the second session on the Friday evening the sharing question steps up a gear. Where the first session moved from personal feelings to the process of thinking, the second session moves to the dimension of faith. The sharing this time is based on a series of interlocking questions, with a progression from the general to the personal and on to the area of practical application and implementation.

The questions are:

a. What does it take to ensure that the Church will continue and will flourish in your parish?

b. Do you want the Church to continue and to flourish in your parish?

c. Why?

d. Who is responsible for ensuring this?

e. How do we go about it?

The **'how to'** question at **e)** above is what we will be working at for the rest of the weekend.

The Saturday Morning Session One: Exploring Parish

Friday evening was about orientation. Through personal feelings, thinking, and sharing faith, the participants and the team of presenters prepared themselves for the work which was to follow on Saturday and Sunday. Saturday begins with the same simple format for the session, and also begins with a sharing question to engage personal feelings and reinforce what is positive: **What are three things you are grateful for in your life as you begin this new day?**

What does Parish Mean to You?

Then there is a sharing question to get people thinking about parish and what it means to them: **When you hear the word parish, what words, phrases, images come to your mind?**

After the sharing, there is a presentation on the twofold nature of parish life: pastoral and administrative, and the two choices for the parish priest: to do all this, pastoral and administrative, on his own, or to involve others. Involving others is best practice. Then two further choices: to involve others as helpers or as partners. A parish pastoral council is a structure for involving others as partners.

A reflection on the characteristics of partnership follows. Just as the parish priest has the option of involving others, and involving them as partners, so too the new parish pastoral council has two choices, to do things by themselves or involve others, and if they involve others, they have the two further choices of involving them as helpers or as partners. Involving others is the main task of the parish pastoral council.

Session Two: Five Qualities of a Catholic Parish

Session Two on Saturday morning begins with a passage of scripture, used as the main vehicle for presenting the theme of the session. The focus is still on parish, but this time the scripture passage is read after the hymn and the prayer, and five qualities of a Catholic parish are explored in the light of this scripture reading.

Scripture Reading: The Transfiguration (Mt 17:1–7)

Six days later, Jesus took with him Peter and James and his brother John and led them up a high mountain where they could be alone. There in their presence he was transfigured: his face shone like the sun and his clothes became as white as the light. Suddenly Moses and Elijah appeared to them; they were talking with him. Then Peter spoke to Jesus. 'Lord', he said, 'it is wonderful for us to be here; if you wish, I will make three tents here, one for you, one for Moses and one for Elijah'. He was still speaking when suddenly a bright cloud covered them with shadow, and from the cloud there came a voice which said, 'This is my Son, the beloved; he enjoys my favour. Listen to him.' When they heard this, the disciples fell on their faces, overcome with fear. But Jesus came up and touched them. 'Stand up', he said, 'Do not be afraid.' And when they raised their eyes they saw no-one but only Jesus.

The five senses:

1. A sense of vocation and of personal responsibility for the faith of our parish.

2. A sense of gladness and joy in being part of the Church in our parish.

3. A sense of freedom to belong to the parish.

4. A sense of the presence of Christ among the people of the parish.

5. A sense of purpose and mission to transform the world around the parish.

The Mass

Mass is celebrated at 12.30 p.m. on Saturday. If there is no major Feast, the Mass of Mary, Mother of the Church, is celebrated. This feast is very appropriate and reinforces the message of who we are as Church as we develop our parish pastoral council. In 1965, at the end of the Second Vatican Council, Pope Paul VI proclaimed the title of Mary, Mother of the Church. In the Irish tradition the title already existed. In *An Leabhar Breac*, compiled early in the fifteenth century, with texts going back as far as the eighth century, we find Our Lady described as '*Muire, Máthair na hEaglaise neamhaí agus talúnda*' – Mary, Mother of the heavenly and earthly Church. In The Stowe Missal from the year 800, in a text which occurs again in *An Leabhar Breac*, the Mass is described as *coinne na hEaglaise neamhaí agus talúnda* – the meeting place of the heavenly and earthly Church.

The Saturday Afternoon
Session Three: Six Priorities for the Church Today

After a Hymn or the L'Arche 'Community Song' , this session is introduced by a Scripture passage:

Scripture Reading: The Marriage Feast of Cana (Jn 2)

On the third day there was a wedding at Cana in Galilee. The mother of Jesus was there, and Jesus and his disciples had also been invited.

When they ran out of wine, since the wine provided for the wedding was all finished, the mother of Jesus said to him 'they have no wine'. Jesus said 'Woman, why turn to me? My hour has not come yet'. His mother said to the servants, 'Do whatever he tells you'.

There were six stone water jars standing there, meant for the ablutions that are customary among the Jews, each could hold twenty or thirty gallons. Jesus said to the servants, 'Fill the jars with water', and they filled them to the brim. 'Draw some out now', he told them 'and take it to the steward'.

They did this; the steward tasted the water and it had turned into wine. Having no idea where it came from – only the servants who had drawn the water knew – the steward called the bridegroom and said 'People generally serve the best wine first and keep the cheaper sort till the guests have had plenty to drink, but you have kept the best wine till now.'

This was the first of the signs given by Jesus, it was given at Cana at Galilee. He let his glory be seen and his disciples believed in him.

Reflection

- About a wedding, but not just about marriage: the story of the Church;
- A crisis story: the crisis of a young couple on their special day;
- At the centre is Jesus; close to the centre is Mary, the Mother of Jesus;
- Mary's command is: 'Do whatever he tells you';
- 'They filled them to the brim';
- How do we know what Jesus is telling us today?

Three sources:

1. Scripture;

2. The teaching and tradition of the Church;

3. The world in which we live (the signs of the times).

Vatican II listened to these three sources and highlighted important priorities for the Church today:

1. Being and building a faith community as a parish;

2. Ecumenism – building bridges with other Christian Churches; alienated Catholics; people of other religions; and people of no faith;

3. Marriage and family Life – the domestic Church;

4. Young people and children – handing on the faith;

5. Empowerment of the laity for leadership;

6. Social teaching on justice, peace, equality: our mission in and to the world.

Participants are asked to prioritise these, as a way of exploring their significance. In the scripture reading on the 'Marriage Feast of Cana', when Jesus asked the servants to fill the jars with water, they filled them to the brim. It was then that the miracle happened. We compare the Church's priority areas with the water jars. It is our job to fill the jars with water – to the brim – bringing our best efforts to the different areas as we work on them. When we have done our bit generously, Jesus will do the rest. The water of our efforts will be turned into wine beyond all our expectations.

The Saturday Afternoon
Session Four: Developing the Agenda

Among the priority areas, the empowerment of the laity stands out, because it is like an umbrella covering the other priority areas. We can talk of the empowerment of the laity for our mission in and to the world, for ecumenism, for marriage and family life, for building faith community and for handing on the faith. For this reason, after the hymn and prayer, this session is introduced through a document on the empowerment of the laity. Instead of talking about the document, copies are given out to participants and they are asked to find a quiet place and read it carefully, marking anything that strikes them as significant. They then meet in their own parish pastoral council groups to examine how themes from their parish survey findings booklet match up with the different priority areas. What is happening here is that parish pastoral councils are beginning to identify themes which will form part of their agenda when they return to their parish.

When the participants return to their own parish pastoral council groups, they will have three things to work on and collate:

1. their marked copy of the document on the empowerment of the laity;

2. five flipchart sheets, each with the name of one of the remaining priority areas;

3. copies of the findings from their parish assembly day.

Process:

- divide into five groups;
- each group is given one of the flipchart sheets;
- each group has copies of their parish assembly findings;
- each group picks out any points from the parish assembly findings which seem to match the particular priority heading on their flipchart sheet. They write these on the sheet.

When each group have completed this process, they report back to the rest of their parish pastoral council, and the groups compare notes and give feedback to each other. They then check the parish assembly findings to see if there is anything that has not been included under the flipchart headings, and consider where they would place these, if they are significant.

When the parish pastoral councils reassemble in the main conference room, it will be pointed out to them that the process they have just taken part in is an important step in gradually gathering together the elements of what will form the overall agenda for their parish pastoral council. It has been cross-referenced with their parish assembly findings, and so is very specific to their own parish.

The Saturday Evening
Session Five: A Spirituality of Hope

After a Hymn or the L'Arche 'Community Song' , this session is introduced by a Scripture passage:

Scripture Reading: The Disciples on the Road to Emmaus (Lk 24: 13–35)

On the first day of the week, two of the disciples were on their way to a village called Emmaus, seven miles from Jerusalem, and they were talking together about all that had happened. Now as they talked this over, Jesus himself came up and walked by their side; but something prevented them from recognising him. He said to them, 'What matters are you discussing as you walk along?' They stopped short, their faces downcast.

Then one of them, called Cleopas, answered him, 'You must be the only person staying in Jerusalem who does not know the things that have been happening there these last few days.' 'What things?' he asked. 'All about Jesus of Nazareth,' they answered, 'who proved he was a great prophet by the things he said and did in the sight of God and of the whole people; and how our chief priests and our leaders handed him over to be sentenced to death, and had him crucified. Our own hope had been that he would be the one to set Israel free. And this is not all: two whole days have gone by since it all happened: and some women from our group have astounded us; they went to the tomb in the early morning, and when they did not find the body, they came back to tell us they had seen a vision of angels who declared he was alive. Some of our friends went to the tomb and found everything exactly as the women had reported, but of him they saw nothing.'

Then he said to them, 'You foolish people! So slow to believe the full message of the prophets! Was it not ordained that the Christ should suffer and so enter into his glory?' Then, starting with Moses and going through all the prophets, he explained to them the passages throughout the scriptures that were about himself.

When they drew near to the village to which they were going, he made as if to go on; but they pressed him to stay with them. 'It is nearly evening,' they said, 'and the day is almost over.' So he went in to stay with them. Now while he was with them at table, he took the bread and said the blessing; then he broke it and handed it to them. And their eyes were opened and they recognised him; but he had vanished from their sight. Then they said to each other, 'Did not our hearts burn within us as he talked to us on the road and explained the scriptures to us?'

They set out that instant and returned to Jerusalem. There they found the eleven assembled together with their companions, who said to them, **'Yes, it is true. The Lord** has risen and has appeared to Simon.' Then they told their story of what had happened on the road and how they had recognised him at the breaking of bread.

The Road to Emmaus story is the story of a crisis: in a way the greatest crisis the disciples could have imagined. Their dreams were shattered. There was no hope. Yet it was the beginning of the greatest renewal. It is the story of Jesus restoring his disciples to hope. His question: **'What matters are you discussing as you walk along?'** must have penetrated to the depths of their despair. They had been overtaken by the negatives, and they couldn't see beyond them. So often we think that what we see is all there is to see, that what we know is all there is to know. There are six pointers in this passage for the followers of Christ, to raise them out of the depths of despair and restore them to hope:

1. **Prayer.** The disciples on the road to Emmaus walked with Christ and talked with Christ, though at first they didn't realise it. Gradually they opened themselves to his presence. We need prayer, to help us to know the presence of Christ, and to allow him to restore us to hope and healing.

2. **The Scriptures.** As they walked along, Jesus opened the scriptures to them, and explained the passages that were about himself. We need the scriptures to enlarge our vision, to be guided beyond the limits of our perception to the bigger picture: lift your eyes to the mountains; extend your horizons from the narrow circle of earth at your feet to the very ends of the earth.

3. **The Eucharist.** The disciples recognised Jesus in the breaking of bread. So often we see the Eucharist as fulfilling

an obligation. A central part of the renewal of the Church is restoring the Eucharist as the source of our energy.

4. **Community.** Our community with one another is the entry-point for Jesus' presence. The joy of the Gospel is in our affirmation of one another, up-building one another, in the gladness we experience in a community of faith and love, in a community of consolation.

5. The importance of the wider community of the Church. When the disciples returned to Jerusalem they found the Eleven assembled with their companions, rejoicing that Jesus was risen and had appeared to Simon. 'Yes, it is true!' We belong in the wider community of the universal Church, which confirms our faith, and guides us through the tradition and teaching of the Apostles.

6. The tradition of the universal Church continually reminds us of the importance of evangelisation: 'accepting the stranger into your home'. We can only keep the faith by handing it on. When we live with hope, nothing is too much; everything is possible.

(For a fuller presentation, see *Think Big, Act Small*, pp. 106–115.)

Session Six: Structures of a Parish Pastoral Council

The greater part of the Saturday evening session is spent on presenting the structures of the parish pastoral council. This necessarily involves a significant amount of detail, covering the establishing of a parish pastoral council, structures of organisation, day to day management, personnel and officers, periods of service and structures of continuity. A great deal of this material will eventually be clarified in diocesan, and possibly even national, guidelines and norms, but it is important for the newly established parish pastoral councils to address the issues and formulate at least the possible shape of the structures which will guide their working relationships.

Structures are not required just so that we may have more rules and regulations. Structures are created for a purpose, and are written down so that when we meet we don't have to re-invent the wheel repeatedly. Some of the purposes of the structures are:

1. to maintain useful routines (for example, number of members; area, gender, age balance; priests' membership *ex officio*; the process of selection, co-option; role of officers like president, chairperson, secretary and deputies).

2. to maintain priorities (for example, prayer, scripture, as an expression of a faith community and to facilitate discernment).

3. to maintain continuity (for example: term of office; renewal of membership by cycle of retirement and replacement; recommended process when a parish priest retires or dies).

Some of the areas covered will be:

Membership
1. Suggested membership in an average sized parish: twelve to fifteen members;

2. The parish priest and any curates to be ex officio members;

3. The first half of the members are selected either at a parish assembly or through a wider parish selection process.

4. The second half of the members are selected by those at numbers two and three above, and drawn from different geographical areas, with gender balance and age balance;

Officers

1. The parish priest will usually be president of the parish pastoral council;

2. The chairperson, whose function is the effective running of meetings, shall be selected by the members for a stated term, of perhaps two years;

3. The secretary, whose function is to take and distribute minutes of meetings, and to communicate with parishioners and others, shall be selected by the members likewise for a stated term, of perhaps two years;

4. For each of these posts a deputy shall be selected, who will automatically take on the leading role at the end of the stated term, at which point new deputies shall be selected.

Period of Service

1. Each member shall serve for a fixed term (for example, three years, allowing for a gradual rotation of members);

2. No member shall serve more than two consecutive terms, but retired members shall be eligible for re-election subsequently;

3. After the initial term of, for example, three years, four members (or another agreed number) shall retire each year in rotation, giving a combination of renewal and continuity; retiring members shall be replaced by a process of selection and/or co-option;

4. Any member failing to attend four consecutive meetings without giving a reasonable explanation shall be deemed to have resigned;

5. Mid-term vacancies shall be filled by co-option.

Agenda

The overall agenda for the parish pastoral council is not something to be identified at random. It should respond to the needs of the parish and of the diocese, and in arriving at it the parish pastoral council should be guided by:

1. the views of the people of the parish as expressed in the initial questionnaire, and in the booklet which followed the questionnaire;

2. the views of the people of the parish gathered in the parish assembly, and expressed in the findings of the assembly and the priorities set there;

3. the priorities of the wider Church, especially in the diocese and in the documents of Vatican II and the statements of the popes and the bishops.

Running of meetings

1. Parish pastoral councils generally meet once a month except for July and August.

2. Each member should have a folder for meetings and be responsible for keeping it up-to-date and keeping track of material from meeting to meeting.

3. Each member is responsible for the health and well-being of the parish pastoral council. Meetings are our meetings, not just the chairperson's or the president's.

4. Choose a good venue – good for reflection, sharing, planning, decision-making. It is important to use basic equipment like a flipchart stand, so that ideas and outcomes may be written up in a way that involves everybody.

5. Meetings should be no more than an hour and a half. This should include ten minutes for prayer, scripture, personal sharing. A parish pastoral council is not a prayer group , but its deliberations should be informed by prayer leading to discernment.

6. There should be fifteen minutes at the end of each meeting to decide the main lines of the agenda for the next meeting.

7. Start on time; finish on time.

8. Confidentiality.

9. A.O.B. should be taken at the start of the meeting. Items listed can be taken if there is time at the end. Otherwise they are rolled over.

10. Minutes should mostly be about decisions made, not a report of what each person has said. Minutes should be communicated to the members and to the parish

community as soon as possible after the meeting. Agenda should be communicated to the parish community.

11. Stick to the agenda. Importance of discipline.

12. The number making up a quorum should be agreed.

13. A sense of humour is a vital part of the process of any meeting and any organisation.

Wrap-up: Questions for Clarification
At the end of the Saturday evening session, reference is made to the sheet from Friday night, and questions for clarification that may not have been addressed in the course of the weekend so far, will now be addressed.

Sunday

The Sunday morning of the residential weekend begins with the celebration of Mass at 8 a.m. There is something very special about Sunday morning. This group of people has worked since Friday evening and all through Saturday. They have studied together, sung together and prayed together. They have shared their faith, their anxieties, their hopes and visions. They have walked together and experienced God's presence as he 'walks with them on the journey of life' (Eucharistic Prayer VN1). They have prepared for this morning's celebration.

Part of the atmosphere is due to Sunday itself. These are people of faith who have lived many Sundays, going to Mass with their families, on dark winter days or in the brightness of an Easter morning.

Dé bheatha an Domhnach tar éis na seachtaine,
Lá breá gréine chun Dia d'agallamh.
Cóirigh do chos go luath chun Aifrinn;
Cóirigh do bhéal chun briathra beannaithe;
Cóirigh do chroí agus díbir an ghangaid as.

Welcome to Sunday after the week,
a fine sunny day to converse with God.
Prepare your foot early to Mass;
Prepare your mouth for sacred words;
Prepare your heart and drive out all bitterness from it.

Following Mass and breakfast, there are two sessions on Sunday morning, leading up to a blessing and missioning ceremony.

At 9.30 a.m. a hymn and an opening prayer lead into a presentation on the Map of Faith Maturity. This is like a follow-through to the faith sharing of Friday night, when people reflected on why they wished the Church to continue and flourish in their parish. At this point they are not just focused on an individual personal reaction: they have been growing in awareness of their leadership role as members of a parish pastoral council, and of the faith dimension of this – it is about leadership of people's lives in faith. Just as the session on Friday night awakened the individual's sense of personal responsibility for handing on the faith, the Map of Faith Maturity addresses the responsibility of the community in handing on the tradition of faith and practice.

Father Michael Paul Gallagher SJ in the 1960s had a remarkable insight: he discovered that Catholic practice in French-speaking Canada had dropped in ten years from 90 per cent practice to less than 40 per cent practice. His insight was that if that had happened in French-speaking Canada, it could happen also in Ireland, which had a similar pattern of high practice levels. He decided to test what had happened in Canada, using the techniques of Sociological surveys. He arranged to survey a sample of parishes in French-speaking Canada where practice had dropped dramatically. But he also surveyed a sample of parishes where practice had remained high. He wanted to know what made the difference. He found a number of factors, including four major indicators. He referred to these factors, taken together, as the 'Map of Faith Maturity'. Where they occurred together in a parish, it was more likely that patterns of practice would be maintained. He also found that these factors fed into each other in an interesting dynamic.

The first significant point on the map was **community.** What was sometimes referred to as a 'me and Jesus' spirituality was not enough. There had to be the support of a community of faith.

The second point was **Prayer.** Faith community expresses itself in prayer: personal prayer, communal prayer, family prayer.

Prayer leads to **Conversion**: conversion to Christ – being set free to believe.

The sign of conversion is **Commitment**: commitment to Christ and to the faith community, and so the cycle continues.

The Map of Faith Maturity

The following diagram represents our development of the Map of Faith Maturity. Every weekend training session added to the understanding of these basics of faith: our understanding was fed and expanded by the interaction of the parish pastoral council groups and their sharing of faith.

Map of Faith Maturity

Faith Community
(not a private spirituality)

Prayer

1. Liturgy (Mass and the Sacraments
2. Personal Prayer
3. Praying with one another (family prayer, shared prayer) Prayer transforming us

Commitment

1. To the people of the community
2. To the concerns of the community, the Church, the world and the poor
3. To the Mission of the Church.
4. Expressed by giving:
   – Time   – Energy
   – Priority

Conversion

1. To the person of Jesus Christ, the Son of the living God.
2. To the presence of Christ: Eucharist, an active presence; where two or three are gathered. Every human person is sacred, and all creation: we're always walking on holy ground.
3. To the power of Christ, to heal, to teach, to forgive, to set free, to save. Jesus is the only one who can save. It is his power we rely on
4. To the Mission of Jesus: to the ends of the earth; to every human person; to transform the world in which we live

The leadership of the parish pastoral council is for a purpose – to lead that cycle of community, prayer, conversion, leading forward into ongoing commitment. There are three things that a parish pastoral council should be continuously working on:

1. **Building a faith community among themselves:**

   The starting point is faith in the Holy Spirit. The parish pastoral council have to experience being a faith community led by the Spirit. This is why prayer and scripture have to be part of the process of the meetings. It is not easy to learn that we are not a committee just making business decisions on an adversarial (competitive) basis. It takes an ongoing commitment to listening and to prayerful discernment, learning to be a forum for the Holy Spirit.

2. **Listening to the community:**

   This has already begun with the survey and the parish assembly, but it has to be ongoing. This is not the same as being a constituency representative, passing on complaints or lobbying from individual parishioners. It is about being inspired by the community, taking responsibility for the pastoral and faith development of the community.

3. **Involving the community:**

   Taking responsibility for the pastoral and faith development doesn't mean that the parish pastoral council should be doing it all themselves. It means finding the people in the parish who have particular gifts and interests and drawing them into the picture. It means continuing communication, sharing the vision. It means ongoing invitation. Across the diocese, in the parish questionnaires, 49 per cent of those who responded said they would be willing to be more involved in the life of the parish. We need to find them and invite them to be involved in specific ways. And everyone needs to be encouraged and affirmed.

Sunday, Session 2: Blessing and Missioning

The final session on Sunday morning, and the concluding session of the whole residential training weekend, is a ceremony of blessing and missioning of the parish pastoral council.

It is introduced by reading the scripture passage from Matthew 28:16–20.

> Meanwhile the eleven disciples set out for Galilee, to the mountain where Jesus had arranged to meet them. When they saw him they fell down before him, though some hesitated. Jesus came up and spoke to them. He said:

> All authority in heaven and on earth has been given to me. Go, therefore, make disciples of all nations; baptise them in the name of the Father and of the Son and of the Holy Spirit, and teach them to observe all the commands I gave you. And remember, I am with you always; yes to the end of time.

This is a very evocative text in the context of the training weekend. It immediately challenges the perception that we are here by accident, that our role in the Church is not significant. Matthew refers to the mountain in Galilee 'where Jesus had arranged to meet them'. Jesus had gathered the apostles, and it is Jesus who has gathered us here this weekend. What Jesus says to his apostles has a resonance for us who are his disciples now. We might even get a bit of encouragement from the fact that Matthew tells us the apostles **'fell down before him, though some hesitated'**. We know the feeling! Jesus speaks then into the company of hesitant disciples. Jesus gives five commands.

The first command of Jesus is **'Go!'** Our temptation is to stay as we are, or even to go back to a more comfortable time ('this is how it was always done'), or at best to move slowly and gradually. Jesus says clearly and simply 'Go' – go forward; leave the comfort zone; launch out into the deep.

The second command of Jesus is **'Make Disciples'**. And he says to make disciples of all nations. We would be inclined to test the waters, to do a pilot project. The apostles probably would have preferred Jesus to say: try working with one of the neighbouring villages and see how you get on: 'Sure, there's no hurry'. Jesus calls on them to lift their eyes to the furthest horizon – to the whole world.

The third command of Jesus is to **Baptise**; 'Baptise them in the name of the Father and of the Son and of the Holy Spirit'. Baptism is not presented here in isolation. The first step is to make disciples; and then Baptism is linked with discipleship. When we say this person is baptised and is now a child of God, we are missing the point. Every created human being is a child of God, whether they know it or not. Baptism makes this person a disciple of Jesus Christ and commissions them to live as a disciple and to spread the kingdom of God. Jesus wants his followers to flood the world with the love, power and wonder of God.

The fourth command of Jesus is to **Teach**: 'Teaching them to observe all the commands I gave you'. The commands of Jesus are to love God with our whole heart, and our whole soul, and our whole mind, and our neighbour as ourselves, and as disciples to love one another as he has loved us: totally and unconditionally.

The fifth command of Jesus is **'Remember I am with you always, to the end of time'**. Jesus asks us for an unlimited vision, to the ends of the earth, but he gives us an unlimited assurance: we do not have to walk alone or work alone – as we bring the Good News of the Gospel to all the nations. He will be with us in every time and in every place – always.

The blessing and missioning of these new parish pastoral councils takes place against the background of that reassuring promise of Jesus.

The room is set up with a circle of chairs for each parish pastoral council. They take their places in their own parish pastoral council groups.

Blessing of Oil

Lord,
you anointed your Son, Jesus Christ,
with the oil of gladness
for the salvation of the world.

We ask you to bless this oil
which will be used to anoint
these parish pastoral council members
for leadership in your Church,

in the name of the Father
and of the Son,
and of the Holy Spirit.
Amen.

Each person is prayed for by the group. One person anoints the person who has been prayed for using the formula:

(*On forehead*) Through this anointing may the Lord fill you with his love;
(*On the hands*) I anoint your hands to heal and to hold, to serve and to bless.

Each person should have the opportunity of both being anointed and of anointing another person.

When each person has been prayed for and anointed, the parish pastoral councils are presented with a lighted candle one by one. The **Blessing of St Fursa** is prayed over each Parish Pastoral Council by one of the team while everyone else extends their hands over them in blessing.

Beannú na gCéadfaithe
'The Blessing of the Senses'

(The Blessing of St Fursa, from the seventh century)

Go raibh cuing reachta Dé ar an ngualainn seo;
Go raibh fiosrú an Spioraid Naoimh ar an gceann seo;
Go raibh comhartha Chríost san éadan seo;
Go raibh éisteacht an Spioraid Naoimh sna cluasa seo;
Go raibh boltanú an Spioraid Naoimh sa tsrón seo;
Go raibh amharc mhuintir neimhe sna súile seo;
Go raibh comhrá mhuintir neimhe sa bhéal seo;
Go raibh obair eaglais Dé sna lámha seo;
Go raibh leas Dé agus na gcomharsan sna cosa seo.
Gurab áit do Dhia an croí seo,
Agus gura le Dia, Athair uile, an duine seo.
Amen.

May the yoke of God's commandments be upon your shoulder;
May the visitation of the Holy Spirit be upon your head;
May the sign of Christ be on your forehead;
May the listening of the Holy Spirit be in your ears;
May the fragrance of the Holy Spirit be in your nose;
May the vision of the people of heaven be in your eyes;
May the conversation of the people of heaven be in your mouth;

May the work of God's church be in your hands;
May the good of God and the neighbours be in your feet.
May your heart be a place for God,
And may this person belong to God, the Father of all.
Amen.

PART THREE

Ongoing Support and Resources

Encouraging, accompanying,
empowering, resourcing
the new parish pastoral councils

Moving Forward – The Energy Within

The previous three chapters, making up Part Two of this book, were about the setting up of the parish pastoral council and the initial training programme. But it is when the parish pastoral council is established that the real challenge begins. That's when the rubber hits the road.

We have a firm belief that the energy for renewing our parishes exists within the parishes themselves. We also believe that the parish pastoral council is the structure that can release that energy and mobilise the resources for the parish for pastoral development.

In this chapter we look at two aspects of the work of the parish pastoral council. The first aspect concerns the working dynamic of the pastoral council; what puts it into gear and drives it forward. The second aspect concerns the range of its most important areas of involvement: where the life of the Church is experienced among the people of the parish. These become priority areas for the work of the parish pastoral council.

Part 1: The Pastoral Council in Action

During the training weekend four actions were identified as the way of being partners in the parish pastoral council. These actions are: **Discern; Decide; Implement; Involve.** Each of these needs to come out of working together as priest and people. And for each of them the parish pastoral council needs further and on-going support and training.

1. Discern

Parish pastoral council meetings should contain a strong element of scripture, prayer and the teaching of the Church in order to discern properly the needs and potential of the people who make up a parish community. These meetings are not, and should never become, prayer meetings. But without prayer, scripture, and a grounding in Church teaching they will not get too far beyond the superficial.

The members of the parish pastoral council need help in being able to enter into this deeper experience of spirituality and to get to the point where each one can take responsibility for leading the prayer, the scripture, and the teaching of the Church. For many this is a very big step that requires training. Without that step being taken true partnership cannot develop.

2. Decide

Everybody's life is full of decisions to be made. Some of these decisions are simple, others are complicated and they need a lot of thought, discussion, and, at times, advice from someone else.

This is also true of a parish pastoral council. The members have to learn to make decisions together, as a group. First of all they need to distinguish the simple decisions that should be made easily from the more serious ones that will take time and effort. The temptation with more difficult decisions is to take short cuts for the sake of saving time. The other failure in making difficult decisions is when the more vocal people make the decisions and others just agree for the sake of peace. Everyone needs to learn to take her or his full part.

The decisions made by a parish pastoral council should be made by consensus rather than by voting. This is a skill that needs to be learned, so that training in this skill will be needed. There are also some techniques which can be developed to facilitate decisions by consensus. Some of these were learned on the residential training weekend, but further training in these should be sought out for the sake of making the best possible decisions as freely as possible.

The most important decisions that a parish pastoral council has to make are about priorities for developing the parish community. These include long-term, medium-term and short term priorities. Identifying them will require experience and guidance.

3. Implement

When decisions have been made it is so important to implement them fully. Partnership means that every member of the parish pastoral council has to take responsibility for implementing decisions. The temptation is to try to offload the implementation to one or another person – often this person tends to be the priest!

Planning together is the key to implementing decisions. This means determining **who** is going to lead the implementation; **how** that person or persons is going to go about it; **when** it will begin and **when** it will be completed; what resources will be needed; and how these resources can be mobilised.

This whole experience of collaborative leadership in the parish, arriving at decisions about the pastoral life of the parish and implementing them, is new to most people. Training in the ways of implementing decisions is necessary so that the parish pastoral council can keep moving forward with freedom and with enthusiasm.

4. Involve

By far the most important questions around the implementation of decisions are **who**, outside of this group, can you involve in implementing decisions taken by the parish pastoral council? And **how** can you recruit them?

In our experience these two questions can be the sticking point for the growth of the leadership potential of the parish pastoral council.

There are strategies and techniques that can be learned, developed and put into practice around these two questions. A parish pastoral council should seek help in developing them. If they don't do this they may end up trying to do everything themselves and the whole project can collapse on this.

Involving others in the implementation of decisions will also mean introducing those people to the process of discerning, deciding, implementing and involving so that more and more parishioners are involved in taking on responsibility for aspects of the parish as a faith community that would otherwise be neglected.

Part 2: Six Priorities for the Church Today

The parish pastoral council in any parish has to work on its agenda and priorities, firstly in the light of the information provided to it by the analysis of the preliminary survey questionnaire and the work of the first parish assembly, and secondly by keeping in touch with the parish and by taking note of communications from the diocese and from the Universal Church.

Naturally, there will be variations in agenda and priorities from time to time and from parish to parish. However, in working with parishes, we identified six priority areas which form a background landscape to the detailed agenda of all the parishes. We proposed these to the new parish pastoral councils as six overarching priorities which should always be kept in view because they are sourced in the documents of Vatican II and in the priorities which surfaced during the various parish assemblies which we facilitated.

These six priorities are:

1. The empowerment of the laity for leadership.

2. Being and building a community of faith in the parish.

3. Marriage and family life: the domestic Church.

4. Children and young people: handing on the faith.

5. Ecumenism: building bridges with other Christian Churches; alienated Catholics; people of other faiths; people of no faith.

6. The social teaching of the Church: our mission in and to the world.

These were presented initially during the residential training weekend, and were developed as part of the ongoing support programme.

Six Priorities for the Parish today

We like to present the six priorities in the form of this visual. At the centre is the empowerment of the laity for leadership in each of the other five. This visual is an important picture of what the Church in the parish is called to be today and in the future. The picture is quite different from the one we have been used to. The way forward is not to try to replicate the past but to respond to the call of Christ in new and creative ways.

The primary call of the parish is to be a community of faith, with Christ at the centre and where there is a place for everyone. The leadership of the parish pastoral council has to be aimed towards this call by constantly building this community in the Lord.

The community of faith is characterised by its faith in the members of the Body of Christ being empowered for co-responsibility with the priests and with each other for the vitality of the whole Community.

The Community of faith has four main responsibilities:

1. To support and develop Marriage and family life as the domestic Church. Pope Francis, in his Letter, *Amoris Laetitia*, describes the parish as 'a family of families' (202).

2. To take its place actively in handing on the great gift of faith to each generation of children and young people, along with their parents and teachers, so that these children and young people can take their place in the community of faith, not just in the future but in the present.

3. To be a community that opens outwards by building bridges towards other Christian Churches; alienated Catholics; people of other religions and cultures; people of no faith.

4. A Community of faith that sees the world we live in as God's creation and that brings God's Word and God's Way to the development of creation and of human living. Pope Francis' letter, *Laudato Si'*, is a magnificent charter for every parish community, opening us up to the ends of the earth.

The role of the parish pastoral council in all of this is pivotal. It can only be done when there is a commitment to empowering others to take leadership and to finding appropriate training for them in their particular roles.

Empowerment of the Laity for Leadership

Baptism, Confirmation and Eucharist are known in the Church as the Sacraments of Initiation. It is through these three great sacraments that each person is drawn into the heart of Christ in his Church and entrusted with the Mission of Christ in the world and to the world.

Through these three sacraments, which most people receive when they are children, each one is empowered to be a disciple of Christ in union with all his other disciples.

In Baptism each one is brought through the saving death of Christ into the new life of his resurrection. Because of this each one is empowered by the Holy Spirit to live the new life of Christ in joy and gladness.

In Confirmation each one is filled with the gifts of the Holy Spirit to be of service to the community of the Church in building her up as the Body of Christ in the world for the transformation of the world in every age.

In the Eucharist each one takes her/his part week by week in the sacrifice of Christ who is constantly saving the world and consecrating it to God. Also in the Eucharist each one is fed with the Body and Blood of Christ in the setting of the community of the Church. Together they are sent out with the full power of Christ to the particular world in which they live in their parish and diocese to be a leaven in that society and to be witnesses to the presence of Christ in the world.

Through these sacraments of initiation each person is already empowered by the Holy Spirit to take her/his part in the life and Mission of the Church. But what is missing?

In 1987, at the Synod of Bishops in Rome, the late Cardinal Tomás Ó Fiaich made the following statement:

The laity of the Church are like a sleeping giant, over seven hundred million strong. They can do immense work for the Kingdom of God, but they must first be fully awakened. It is sad to have to admit that the laity in most parishes are still a largely untapped resource.

That is what the parish pastoral council is for – to awaken the sleeping giant in each of our parishes. The power is already there. What is missing is that this power needs to be released by the Community of the Church in meaningful and constructive ways so that the gifts of each person can be used for the good of all. That is what is meant by the empowerment of the laity. That is the major task of the parish pastoral council.

Being and Building a Community of Faith as a Parish

Most people today belong to a variety of communities each of which meets different needs of individuals. The Christian community of the parish is no longer the only one, and for many people no longer the main one especially at a social level.

Today we have to reclaim community as central to the living of our faith in Christ. It is not a private relationship with Christ that is somehow fed by the wonderful gifts of the Church. What we have is a community of faith among whom Christ lives and in which each one is nourished into a personal relationship with Christ that gives fresh meaning to life. In all that we do as Catholics we have to know that it is coming from the fact of belonging to this community as a witness to the world.

The Irish American Jesuit, Fr Chuck Gallagher, had a saying: 'you cannot have the faith without the faithful'. It is in a living faith community that faith thrives. In the early Irish

Church, both within the monasteries and in the community surrounding the monasteries, the warmth of the sense of community was expressed by the word *muintearas*, the quality of belonging, of being a family.

For us as Catholics this sense of belonging, of being a family, is expressed particularly in our celebration of the Eucharist and the other sacraments of the Church. And one of the main purposes of the Eucharist and other sacraments is to build us continuously into a deeper sense of Communion with one another in Christ.

This does not happen automatically. It has to be made happen by how we actually celebrate these very special occasions. This is true particularly when we come to the question of Sunday Mass. A real deficiency in our Catholic spirituality is the mentality of getting this done as quickly and painlessly as possible. A great starting point for renewal would be to dedicate an hour each Sunday to the Mass. This gives time for three essentials of the Mass:

1. Celebration

2. Participation

3. Hospitality

When we are not rushing things we can then celebrate and not just get through it. We can attend to the joy of making each Sunday a fresh start to a new week in our relationship with God, with ourselves, and with each other.

When we are not rushing we have time to take part in everything that the Mass is about: the prayer responses; the singing together; the hope that God's word brings us; the awesome miracle of Christ's sacrifice; the extraordinary gift of communion; the privilege of being commissioned to be God's people in the world for the week ahead.

When we are not rushing we have time to meet other people and build friendships that encourage us or that bring comfort to others. It doesn't have to take all our time. But it does need some of our time to really let the Mass and the other sacraments unite us with one another and with Christ.

Marriage & Family Life: The Domestic Church

On 19 March 2016 Pope Francis issued a letter entitled *Amoris Laetitia*, on love in the family. It took three years to write this letter. It began with a worldwide consultation of Catholics and their experiences of Marriage and family Life. This was followed up with two month-long synods of Bishops at which many lay people were present in 2014 and 2015. Then there were six months of hard work by Pope Francis and his team to bring it all together into a one hundred and fifty-nine page letter.

It is a thoughtful articulation of our Catholic faith and how we believe in the vital importance of Marriage and family as core elements in the presence of Christ in the world for the salvation of the world. That is the meaning of the wonderful title of Domestic Church.

There was a time when Marriage and family were almost synonymous. That is no longer the case. There are many different combinations of families in our world and in our Church. We have to reverence all of them as sacred because of the bonds of love that bind them and because of the Sacrament of Baptism that identifies them as belonging to us as a community.

Marriage

In his letter, *Amoris Laetitia*, Pope Francis reaffirms the Catholic teaching that the Sacrament of Marriage is the marriage of a woman and man that is entered into in the context of the faith community. This is an extraordinary act of faith – to place the love relationship of husband and wife alongside the other great sacraments of Christ with equal reverence.

When a couple get married they pledge their love to each other in fidelity and in perpetuity. It is this pledge by each of the two people that establishes them as a sacrament. It's not so much that they receive a Sacrament. They become a sacrament, making Christ present by their love for each other.

A very important part of this sacrament though is that, just as they pledge their love to each other, so we as the community of the Church pledge to support them in that love in every way that is possible. They cannot do it on their own. We need to strengthen our support systems in order to live up to this pledge.

Similarly when parents bring their child for Baptism they promise to bring their child up in the faith. Part of this sacrament though is that we too, as a faith community, promise to support them in every way they will need so that they can fulfil their promise. They cannot do it on their own without the active support of the faith community.

> The main contribution to the pastoral care of families is offered by the parish, which is the family of families, where small communities, ecclesial movements and associations live in harmony. (*Amoris Laetitia*, 202)

Children and Young People: Handing on the Faith

There are three sources of formation for children and young people. This is true for them at every level of their lives. And it is true for them in the formation of their faith.

The Home

Parents are the primary teachers of their children in everything that is good in human living. They teach mainly by example. They also teach by their love. Parents/grandparents/extended family help them to know most of all that they are lovable and are loved. They will get this experience in many other ways through their lives. But it is in the home that they need to get it mostly so that they will be able to believe it all through their lives. It is in the home also that children and young people are taught a sense of responsibility for others, beginning with the rest of the family. That is why discipline is so important in family life. They learn the responsibility of gratitude, of kindness, of sharing, of loving others. And it is in the home that children and young people learn the intimacy of God's presence and love. Family prayer is such an important part of this learning.

The School

School is geared mostly towards teaching knowledge. This is done by people who are trained for this purpose. But the school also teaches the art of living with others. Again, discipline is such an important part of this learning which in turn is so important for life. Through knowledge a person's mind and heart are opened up to the wonder of life and of the world.

Our Catholic schools are geared to teach knowledge within the ethos of the Catholic Church. This involves teaching knowledge of the faith. It also includes teaching the values of the faith including reverence for oneself, for every person, and for all creation. Forgiving others and being forgiven are other vitally important values that the school teaches. And, of course, the Catholic school through its schedule teaches the presence of God because of its times of prayer in class and in assemblies.

The Parish Community/Diocese
Children and young people are also formed by the community in which they live and by the society of which they are a part. The Catholic community has to participate actively in this formation of faith. The faith community of the parish and the diocese teaches the story of faith that has been handed on from generation to generation. It has the story and the memory of those who have gone before us. It needs to celebrate that story and memory and bring the children and young people into that celebration. The community also teaches the practice of faith, especially in the celebration of the Eucharist week by week and day by day. It is so important that children and young people are involved in the Eucharistic celebration as an active part of it. This is also true of the other sacraments that are core to our life as Catholics. The community of the parish is also an experience of belonging to a huge variety of people from every background and every age of life. Young people need this experience if they are to grow into healthy, mature adults. And the diocese is a very important part of this maturing that opens our children and young people up to the world in which we live in a different way than they will have from any other source.

These three sources of formation in faith for children and young people are distinct from each other. But they need to be working together and supporting each other. To a great extent the leadership of the faith community, the parish pastoral council, has the main responsibility to ensure that this happens.

Ecumenism

Building Bridges with other Christian Churches;
with alienated Catholics; with people of other Religions;
with people of no faith.

All the way through this book we have been referring to the Church primarily as community. That is the essential nature of the Church at every level, especially at the level of the parish. The task of the parish is to be a community of faith and to constantly build a community of faith.

People often think of community as a group of people who are closed in on themselves in various ways. Many communities become like that. And many Christian communities develop like that.

However when we speak of the Church as a community we envisage a community that opens outward to all of humanity and all of creation. That is the vision of the Catholic Church as proposed by the Second Vatican Council and by so much of the teaching and activity of the Catholic Church's leadership over the past fifty years and more.

The Prayer of Jesus

In chapter seventeen of St John's Gospel we are put in touch with the continuous prayer of Jesus for his Church and from the heart of his Church.

> May they all be one. Father, may they be one in us, as you are in me and I am in you, so that the world may believe it was you who sent me. I gave them the glory you gave to me, that they may be one as we are one. With me in them, and you in me, may they be so completely one that the world will realise that it was you who sent me and that I have loved them as much as you loved me. (Jn 21–23)

These passionate words of Christ give a very clear statement of what he wants for us as his Church in every age: our unity with one another. And they clearly show the purpose of our unity – **'so that the world may believe'**. Only when all of humanity and all of creation are gathered into one in Christ will the kingdom of God be fulfilled.

The parish pastoral council needs to take the leadership in building this unity with all those who live with them in their local area, keeping in mind these four headings:

1. Other Christian Churches in the area with whom we have a particular relationship through our shared Baptism and from whom we can get new inspiration and strength.

2. Alienated Catholics from whom we could learn so much that would refresh our faith.

3. People of other religions with whom we share a common belief in God even if in a different way.

4. People of no faith with whom we share a common humanity and with whom, as with all the other individuals and communities, we could work together to benefit the world in which we live.

Social Teaching of the Church
Our Mission in the World
Our Mission to the World

A Different Way of Seeing Things
There is no doubt that the world we live in is in bad shape in so many ways. The truth is that it always was and always will be suffering from many of the same realities of war and destruction as we have today.

When Jesus looked at that world he could see all that was wrong with it and 'he felt sorry for them (the people around him)'. But then he said 'The harvest is great'. He could see all the goodness of the people; all the wonders of their lives; all the possibilities that were there. All they needed was for someone to believe in them, to love them, and to show them the way. That was his mission. It is now also the mission of the Church, our mission, in every generation and in every community of the world.

Social Teaching of the Church

For the past two thousand years every generation of the Church has reflected deeply on the questions of their times. They have done this in prayer. They have also done it, rooted in Christ, in the Scriptures and as he walks with and in the Church in every age.

This deep reflection was done by monks; by theologians; by the bishops and Pope; and by the faithful in every place. This reflection has been gathered at different times into official teaching through the councils and synods of Pope and bishops as well as in encyclical letters by the popes and diocesan letters by the local bishops. A vast amount of wisdom has thus been gathered. Often this mission has to be restated for new times and responding to new questions. At various stages of the Church particular emphases needed to be highlighted. This meant that other important truths seemed to be placed in the background. The Church's story has been one of the Church constantly reshaping itself for its own time.

Main elements of the Social Teaching of the Church

There are clear elements that come through the ongoing social teaching of the Church.

1. The dignity of every human person made in the image and likeness of God.

2. The personal human relationships made in the image of the Trinity, especially marriage and family.

3. The proper ordering of society to cater especially for the poor and marginalised.

4. Our human relationship with all of creation as guardians of creation so that it can flourish according to God's plan and for the real good of humanity as we care for our common home. This part of our faith was powerfully presented to us, and to the world, by Pope Francis on 24 May 2015 with the publication of his encyclical letter, *Laudato Si'*.

Our Christian lives are developed and lived around these four elements. We need to be open to the wonderfully rich teaching that is here. We need to order our lives as responses to this teaching; we need to build our parish community as a people who are known by these qualities; and we need prayer if we are to enter into the privilege of being at the heart of God's continuing work in the world.

Our mission as Christians in the world is to live the values of these four elements of the social teaching of the Church in every way we can in our personal, family, work, and social life.

Our Mission to the World is, as a parish community, to challenge the society in every way necessary to keep these four elements at the forefront of decisions that are made politically and socially.

Support Documents

As part of the support programme for parish pastoral councils, we wrote a working document for each of the six priority areas. These are now available as booklets:

1. Empowerment of the Laity for Leadership;

2. Being and Building a Community of Faith;

3. Marriage and Family Life – The Domestic Church;

4. Children and Young People – Handing on the Faith;

5. Ecumenism – Building Bridges;

6. Catholic Social Teaching – Mission in and to the World.

These booklets are available from:
paddi@continuousprayer.net

This is not a commercial enterprise, but there will be a charge to cover printing costs and post and packaging.

The Church in a State of Mission

Throughout this book we have been discussing the development of parish pastoral councils. Yet, if we are asked what this book is about, what this whole project is about, we can confidently say: it is not about the pastoral council. Because the pastoral council is never an end in itself. The pastoral council is about the parish, and the diocese. It is about pastoral development, catechesis and evangelisation.

> The parish community is the focal point of faith development in all its forms. Initial proclamation, Christian initiation, religious education, new evangelisation and theological reflection all find a home within the parish community. The task of catechesis and faith development generally underpins the other principal tasks of the parish. In parish, the adult members of the local faith community, together with their children and young people, seek to support one another in faith and to grow continually in understanding, sharing and living that faith.(Irish Episcopal Conference: *Share the Good News*, pp. 190–191.)

The vision of *Share the Good News* is for a fully formed and empowered Church community, guided by the Holy Spirit.' (*Share the Good News*, p. 190).

The formation and empowerment of a parish faith community cannot be achieved from outside. It needs to be stimulated from within. The parish pastoral council is uniquely placed to contribute to that formation and empowerment, in unity with the parish priests who themselves are part of the parish pastoral council, and supported by the diocese, encouraging, recognising, resourcing and accompanying them.

Building up the local Church community from within is not something separate from reaching out in evangelisation. It is all part of the same process.

> A mutual enrichment can take place between the mission *ad intra* (within the Church) and the mission *ad extra* (beyond the Church). Particular situations require particular responses, but all evangelising action should be seen as a unity. (*Share the Good News*, p. 60.)

The extraordinary missionary energy of the early Irish Church flowed from a Church at home that was a vibrant community (muintearas), nourished by the Word of God, and confident in belonging to the communion of saints: the Mass was seen and experienced as 'the meeting-place of the heavenly and earthly Church' (The Stowe Missal, AD 800). A similar confidence marked the equally remarkable missionary movements which reached out from the Irish Church in the twentieth century.

On the Sunday of the residential training weekend, the two main sessions are built on what energises the Church from within (the Map of Faith Maturity) and the missioning of the Apostles by Jesus in Matthew 28 ('Go, therefore; make disciples of all the nations').

The Map of Faith Maturity includes the Church as faith community (the Church *ad intra*), but it opens out to the world which is hungry for the Word of God. Conversion is to the person of Christ, to the presence of Christ, to the power of Christ, to the mission of Christ. Commitment is to the people of the Church, to the concerns of the Church, to the mission of the Church. The building of the faith community of the Church leads directly to evangelisation. That is what the Church is about.

On the 12 September 1962, a month before the opening of the Second Vatican Council, Pope Saint John XXIII broadcast a memorable radio message looking forward to the Council. He introduced the Council as a continuation of our Lord's commandment:

Go, therefore, make disciples of all the nations; baptise them in the name of the Father and of the Son and of the Holy Spirit, and teach them to observe all the commands I gave you. (Mt 28: 19–20)

Pope John XXIII was drawing on an approach proposed by Cardinal Suenens (at the Pope's request). Cardinal Suenens concluded the document he submitted to Pope John with this paragraph:

If I might be permitted to express one wish at the end of this note, it is that the Council may be above all a pastoral, that is an apostolic Council. What an immense benefit it would be for the Church if it could define the broad outlines of how the whole Church could be put into a state of mission, and at all levels: lay people, clergy, bishops and Roman Congregations! What a splendid Pentecostal grace this would be for the Church, just as our beloved Head wished for with so much heart and Christian hope!' (*Vatican II By Those Who Were There*, Geoffrey Chapman, p. 94.)

Pope John accepted the proposal. It was first supported by a number of influential cardinals, and then approved by all the bishops in council. The Second Vatican Council became a pastoral and apostolic council. The idea of a new evangelisation is rooted in Vatican II, and was taken up by all the popes that followed.

It is in this context that the role of parish pastoral councils can be particularly significant.

To fulfil their role, parish pastoral councils need to be effective. It is not enough to develop a pastoral council in a parish and then let it just sit there, at best a decorative addition to the parish structure, or at worst just a list of names to be added to the diocesan statistics.

The dynamic of pastoral development through collaborative ministry and the Parish Pastoral Council is one which begins from the community and flows back to the community in a continuous cycle. The cycle has to be established and promoted consciously, because the natural inertia of human nature and parish life will tend to slow it down or even bring it to a stop. (*Think Big, Act Small*, p. 57)

The tendency to slow down is as old as the Church itself. In the aftermath of the crucifixion and death of Jesus, Peter and the Apostles were shocked and confused. There is a lovely story in John, chapter 21:

Later on, Jesus showed himself again to the disciples. It was by the Sea of Tiberias, and it happened like this: Simon Peter, Thomas called the Twin, Nathanael from Cana in Galilee, the sons of Zebedee and two more of his disciples were together. Simon Peter said, 'I'm going fishing'. They replied, 'We'll come with you'. They went out and got into the boat but caught nothing that night.

There's something very endearing about this picture of Peter and his friends reverting to type. When we're disillusioned we don't have the energy for new initiatives. We want to do what we're used to, what we're good at. Peter says: 'I'm going fishing', because fishing was what he knew about. It was what he was most confident about. In spite of all that, it wasn't a good outing: they caught nothing that night.

Once again in that crisis situation Jesus appears. At first he's just the stranger on the shore, but when he tells them to cast the net to starboard, they are overwhelmed by the catch of one hundred and fifty-three big fish, and they realise: 'It is the Lord'.

In the first enthusiasm of setting up a parish pastoral council, we can easily forget how new this all is. Neither priests nor people are on familiar ground. It may feel as if we've been up all night and caught nothing.

This is why support is so vital. Even after a good experience of the initial training a new parish pastoral council can settle into a routine where meetings happen, relationships are quite positive, members become comfortable, and very little happens beyond the meeting or beyond the group.

That is not due to a lack of good will, but the members need stimulus, support and guidance to encourage them to push the boat out (*Duc in Altum*) and begin to involve other people and explore ways of mobilising the wider parish community to take on responsibility for the key areas of parish life.

The inspiration for that has to come from the diocese, which has the perspective and the authority and resources to involve the parish pastoral councils (including the parish priests) in developing their own pastoral plan in unity with an overall diocesan pastoral plan. This is not a short-term project. The diocese will be involved in a continuing programme of support, accompanying the parishes, encouraging them, and providing them with practical resources and in-service training and formation. This is a big commitment from the diocese, requiring a courageous investment of time and money. It is a worthwhile investment, because it is an investment in the mission of the Church.

More important than the investment of time and money is the investment of faith. The diocesan and parish community depends on faith in the Risen Christ, and on faith in the presence of the Risen Christ in his Church. It depends on faith in the Holy Spirit and on faith in the presence and power of the Holy Spirit in the community of the Church and in each of its members: 'To each is given the shining forth of the Spirit for the common good' (1 Cor 12:7).

One of the key roles of leadership in the Church is to affirm the faith of the people of the Church, to enable them to trust in the power of the Holy Spirit working in them since their Baptism and Confirmation. This is particularly true of the leadership of the priest in the parish.

Bishop Donal Murray spoke of this at a priests' retreat in Ards Monastery in Donegal in the summer of 2014:

'The big challenge for the ordained priest is to become more fully aware of his role in awakening people's awareness of who they are – sharers in the priesthood of Christ.' The priesthood of the laity and the ordained priest are not in opposition: the ordained priest is at the service of unfolding the baptismal grace of all Christians.

Bishop Murray spoke not only of Baptism, but of the Eucharist and of the eucharistic community:

The community gathered for the Eucharist is gathered by what is deepest within them, the voice of God whom we encounter in our hearts. We are called to offer our capacities to God – that is the source of our strength. Belonging to an institution or a club or an association however important and absorbing, is an involvement which is partial and limited. Belonging to the community of those called out by God's word involves the whole of ourselves.

Faith needs the support of prayer, a hugely significant resource both of the parish and of the diocese. At the time of the Second Vatican Council, when Pope Saint John XXIII was considering what to do for the renewal of the Church, he began with prayer. Here is his lovely prayer to the Holy Spirit:

Divine Spirit,
renew your wonders in our time,
as though for a new Pentecost,
and grant that the holy Church,
preserving unanimous and continuous prayer,
together with Mary the mother of Jesus,
and also under the guidance of Saint Peter,
may increase the reign of the Divine Saviour,
the reign of truth and justice,
the reign of love and peace.

PART FOUR

A Strategic View

The development of parish pastoral councils is the opportunity for a new beginning, not only in the individual parishes, but in the relationship of the parishes within the diocese and of the diocese with the parishes.

Building a Profile of the Local Church

In chapter three we gave some information on the origins of the process we used in assisting parishes to develop a parish pastoral council. In particular, we discussed the role of the parish survey, and gave a copy of the survey questionnaire which we used.

The background to this kind of questionnaire is what is generally referred to as strategic planning. Put very simply it means, for a business or a community group or a parish, looking at where we are now, looking at where we might want to go in the future, and finding some basic steps which could help us to make the journey. Frank Dolaghan gave a very succinct presentation of this concept in chapter two of *Think Big, Act Small*, based on his experience as a strategic planning consultant.

The questionnaire is one handy way to establish a baseline picture of where the parish is now, as perceived by the parishioners themselves, and also to begin to sketch an outline vision of how the parish might develop into the future.

When the responses to the survey questions were analysed, they were presented in a printed A4 booklet, and became an important building block for pastoral planning in the parish and for establishing the agenda for the new parish pastoral council.

At that early stage we thought of the survey outcomes only as a tool within the individual parish – a useful tool in the hands of each parish pastoral council. However, as the number of parishes grew, and we found ourselves looking at the survey outcomes for twenty-one parishes, spread across rural and urban parishes, and on both sides of the border (Northern Ireland and the Irish Republic), we realised that we had a sample of several thousand responses, creating a useful overview across the Diocese of Derry. The sample provides a significant indicator of the profile of parishes in the Derry Diocese. For other dioceses it is not a direct indicator, but the averaging out of responses can suggest at least an illustrative model of what might be learned from similar surveys carried out locally.

Some other dioceses have achieved a diocesan overview by carrying out a diocese-wide listening exercise, where again a sample of several thousand can give a dependable indicator of attitudes across the diocese.

We have averaged out the responses from the twenty-one parishes. The detail of the average percentage responses is given in the tables in Appendix One. Here we simply list the topics covered in the five sections of the questionnaire, and add our own reflections on the outcomes from each section.

Most of the surveys were done during the years 2012 and 2013. A couple of them come from a slightly earlier period. All the parishes are in the Diocese of Derry and add up to almost half the parishes in the diocese. Throughout these parishes, 17,215 people filled in this survey.

Background Statistics

Before dealing with the five sections of the questionnaire and the detailed results it is worth highlighting the profile of those who answered the survey in terms of gender and age groupings. The details of both of these can be seen under section five in this chapter.

Gender
- **58.6%** were **female**
- **39.7%** were **male**
- **1.7%** did not indicate gender
- **14,746** people completed this question

Age Groups
- **39.72%** were in the age group **31–55**
- **25.00%** were in the age group **56–70**
- **11.8%** were in the age group **12–18**
- **11.1%** were over **70**
- **10.5%** were in the age group **19–30**
- **14,800** people completed this question

These statistics give us some indication of the average composition of our congregations at weekend Masses. Children were not included among those who filled in surveys and need to be factored into the overall composition of our congregations.

It is probably fairly accurate that most of our congregations are made up of more women than men, although it is reasonably close. And our congregations are mostly made up of those aged thirty-two to seventy – as well as, of course, children.

The responses that follow are very significant for the individual parishes. But, even more importantly they give a real picture of the diocese, a picture that could well have relevance for many other dioceses.

Section 1: Relationships and Involvement in the Parish

In this section the questionnaire begins with the people who make up the parish community and consequently the diocese. This is by far the most important part of the Church! We look at their relationships with each other under various headings and their levels of involvement within the parish. We also look at the levels of care we have for different groupings.

1. The quality of relationships between priest(s) and people.

2. Relationships between the people and the schools.

3. The work of parish organisations.

4. Co-operation between parish organisations.

5. Involvement of women in the parish.

6. Involvement of men in the parish.

7. The process of decision making in the parish.

8. Involvement of youth in the parish.

9. The level and range of parish based social activities.

10. Relationships with other Christian Churches locally.

11. Support for families in the parish.

12. Support for bereaved people.

13. Support for elderly people.

14. Support for people with disabilities.

15. Support for sick people.

16. Support for marriages in difficulties.

17. Support for teenagers and young people.

18. Support for single adults in the parish.

19. Relationships among parishioners.

The nineteen questions in this section refer to most of the important areas of relationship and involvement in a parish community and consequently in the local Church of the diocese. There is a lot to take heart from here. There are also many challenges that should become priorities.

How to Read the Average Percentages

Where we find the responses going between **Good** and **Very Good**, there is a lot of positive energy to call on. For example, the first question is:

The quality of relationship between Priest(s) and People is: the responses are **46.9% Very Good** and **36.6% Good**.

This might surprise many people because the public perception, wherever it comes from, is that this relationship is not all that good. Yet **83.5%** of people say that it is good. We need to take a lot of encouragement from that and, as we rejoice in it, build on it. Of course there are **13.56%** who see that relationship as only **Fair** or **Poor** and these also have to be listened to.

The same is true with the question of **the relationship of the people and the schools**. The overall level of satisfaction is high – **67.4%** go between **Very Good** and **Good**. Here the one to look at is those who marked **Don't Know: 17.3%**. Why would they mark that one?

Where we find that the responses go between **Good** and **Fair** there is a clear indication that something needs to be done. An example of this is the question: **The Process of Decision-making in the parish is: 33.7%** said it is **Good** but **20.3%** said it is **Fair**. And **23.6%** said **Don't Know**. There would seem to be a fair lack of transparency in this one that needs to be dealt with and improved.

This same trend is there in the question: **Involvement of Youth in the parish is: 28.1%** said it is **Good**; **26.7%** said it is **Fair**; and **19.1%** said it is **Poor**. What can be done about this is a very big question. But it urgently needs to be dealt with.

Support for Various Groupings of People

The second part of this section is about the ways that people see the level of support for groupings like the sick; the elderly; those with disabilities; those who are bereaved etc.

Generally the level of support is seen as reasonably good but with many of them it could be and needs to be improved on.

However it is here that the level of **Don't Know** is significant. This is particularly true in two of them. Firstly, on the question of: **Support for Marriages in difficulties is: 51.2%** marked **Don't Know**. This can be because of lack of information or it can be because of lack of personal interest. Or it can come from a mentality of privacy – 'that's their own business'. Of course we cannot interfere in people's lives. But marriage difficulties can be one of the most traumatic experiences that people go through. It's a situation that needs all the support and consolation that a Community can give. Otherwise it is a very lonely place to be.

The other question in this section that needs particular attention is: **Support for Single Adults in the Parish is:** The responses here go from **Good 21.4%** to **Fair 18.7%** to **Poor 10.1%**. However, **43.4%** marked **Don't Know**.

Single life is hardly ever mentioned or even thought about. Single people are not generally included socially. This is so often highlighted by married people who lose a spouse to death or separation. Their experience is generally that they are not part of the Community like they were when they had a wife or husband. And the **Vocation of the Single Person** is like news to most people. The Parish Community has the responsibility to change this and include single people not just for their sake but for the sake of the health and well-being of the whole Community. The Diocese has a great responsibility in this also.

Each one of the nineteen questions and the responses to them deserve examination at both parish and diocesan level. Unless we are dealing with the needs and the potential of the people we are missing the heart of the faith community.

Section 2: Sacraments in the Parish

The questions for this section are all focused on people's experience of the arrangements and supports within their parish for the various sacraments and other things associated with these. These questions do not touch on the theology or spirituality of the sacraments. However the responses can lead to recognising the great need that parishes have of ongoing input on the significance of each of the Sacraments for the faith development of the whole parish.

1. Baptism arrangements and support.

2. First Holy Communion arrangements.

3. Arrangements for Confirmation.

4. Support for Marriage preparation.

5. Arrangements for Marriage.

6. Support for couples after marriage.

7. Arrangements for funerals.

8. Arrangements for Sacrament of the Sick.

9. Times of weekend Masses.

10. Participation by lay people in Masses.

When we look at these results a number of trends appear. The first of these is that, although there are four possible answers, two of these stand out in eight of the ten pages, namely **No Change Needed** and **Unable to Comment**. The other two possible answers feature hardly at all in these eight.

The high level of the response **No Change Needed** certainly indicates a lot of satisfaction in most of the parishes with how things are being managed. That is a real strength in the parishes and for the diocese. But this can also prove a weakness because changes are becoming more necessary with the increasing shortage of priests. Changes in the arrangements for all of the sacraments are also becoming necessary as we become more aware of the communal nature of each of the sacraments.

Unable to Comment features greatly in this section. We could easily miss the significance of this. People are unable to comment on things for a variety of reasons. It may be because they are not informed about them. Greater communication is then needed to give people this information.

Or it could be that people are unable to comment on things because they don't see those things as having any relevance to them. Many of the sacraments have to do with children and young people. Parishioners can easily see Baptism as having to do with parents of new babies. And that's not them! Or people can see First Communion and Confirmation as being the responsibility of the schools with nothing to do with them. And so on.

This highlights the importance of good instruction that can lead to everyone recognising that these sacraments are primarily the responsibility of the parish community and they should be celebrated within the context of that community.

Unable to Comment can also indicate a lack of interest. This easily develops when we think of the practice of our faith as a private thing between God and each of us. We do all that is expected of us and it's up to others to do the same.

Specific Trends

In the three questions around the **Sacrament of Marriage**, **No Change Needed** and **Unable to Comment** are almost equal in strength. This is different from most of the others where **No Change Needed** is almost double the one on **Unable to Comment**.

1. **Support for Marriage Preparation: No Change Needed 44.2%; Unable to Comment 41.2%**

   Arrangements for Marriage: No Change Needed 45.9%; Unable to Comment 42.1%

Support for Couples after Marriage: No Change Needed 30.2%; Unable to Comment 45.5%

So much depends on the quality of this relationship in our parishes as highlighted by Pope Francis in *Amoris Laetitia*. Of course the couples themselves have the primary responsibility for their Marriage. But, in accepting couples to the Sacrament of Marriage, the community of the Church both in parish and diocese pledges to support them in every way possible so that they can grow into signs of great love in their family and community. In practice little support is offered. And this is growing less.

On the question of support for couples after Marriage **21.2%** said this **Could be Improved**. This is quite a substantial call for change.

2. A question that is often talked about in parishes concerns the times of weekend Masses. It's interesting on this question that, in the average percentages for twenty-one parishes **71.2%** say **No Change Needed**; **15.9%** say **Could be improved**.

   This question is becoming more urgent today with the shortage of priests. Many changes to times will have to be made. A lot of instruction is called for to restore the sense of the vital importance of the Eucharist, not just for the nurturing of the individual, but for the strengthening of the faith community.

3. Even though **62.4%** of people responded **No Change Needed** to the question of participation by lay people in Masses, **22.3%** responded that it **Could be Improved**. This percentage of concern needs to be taken seriously.

Section 3: Parish Resources

There are just seven questions in this section. These questions focus on:

1. The people of the parish as the single most important resource.
2. Good information and communication within the parish.
3. Ownership of the parish by the people as shown in the willingness to be involved and in financial contributions.

When these three resources are strong the future of the parish is assured. If any of them are weak the future will be more difficult.

1. Involvement of laity essential part of parish life.
2. Prepared to become more involved in work of the parish.
3. Am well informed about parish activities, events and news.
4. Find the weekly bulletin helpful.
5. I contribute regularly to Church collections.
6. I am eligible for and have entered the Gift Aid/Covenant scheme.
7. I understand and know where my contributions are being used.

1. One of the outstanding features of the responses in this section is that **88.5%** said they find the weekly parish bulletin/newsletter helpful. Let all parish secretaries take a bow!

   What this highlights for us is that people really appreciate regular information about their parish and they deserve it.

Good communication within the parish cannot be emphasised enough.

2. **79.6%** of respondents say that they see the involvement of the laity as an essential part of parish life.

   That is a very strong endorsement for the parish and the diocese to move forward confidently in developing lay involvement. It is important to realise that this endorsement is for lay involvement as **essential**, not just as advisable.

3. **49%** of people say that they are prepared to be more involved in the work of the parish.

   This will probably surprise many people. One of the stresses in many parishes is to get people to become involved. It very often falls back on the same people to do everything.

   The questions need to be asked about how we ask people; what we ask them to get involved in; how do we support them in their involvement; what kind of training do we give people for the kind of involvement that needs training.

   Almost half of those who responded say they are willing for more involvement. The leadership of the parish and diocese needs to find the ways of reaching them.

4. **87%** say that they contribute regularly to Church collections. That would seem higher than many people would think!

   However only **53%** say that they understand how and where their contributions are being used. **53%** is quite high but it leaves a real gap of information to be filled. **32.6%** say they **Don't Know** where their contributions are being used while **13.5%** are **Unable to Comment**.

5. The question about Gift Aid is specific to the north of Ireland. When people are paying taxes and they sign the

Gift Aid form the parish gets a return of taxes on their parish contributions.

Section 4: Parish in the Future

In this section people are invited to look ahead five years and identify various things they would like to see in their parish by then.

This is done in two ways. Firstly they look at some services they would like to see developed by then. They are given a list of these and asked to tick as many or as few as they wish. Then they are asked to identify the kind of community they want to see under the headings of various qualities. Again they may tick as many or as few as they want.

The outcome of this is a vision statement written by the community of the parish for the parish. A consequence of this is that it is also a vision statement for the diocese written by a large sample of the faithful, **14,000–15,000** of them. It needs to be listened to by the leadership.

There is no attempt made in this section to indicate how any of these things can be developed. It is the purpose of the parish pastoral council to find the ways and to find the people to bring all of this about. It is also the task of the parish pastoral council to empower these people as leaders so that they in turn can do the same for others.

1. An active parish pastoral council.

2. Adult religious education programmes.

3. Supports for marriage & family life.

4. Widespread family prayer.

5. Involvement of youth in the life of the Church.

6. Links with other Christian Churches locally.

7. Greater involvement of people in parish organisations.

8. I would like to see a vibrant community which: Deepens faith.

9. I would like to see a vibrant community which: Hands on the Faith.

10. I would like to see a vibrant community which: Encourages all vocations.

11. I would like to see a vibrant community which: Is an inclusive community. (gender, social status, age, etc.)

12. I would like to see a vibrant community which: Is a caring community.

There are two columns in this section that read: **Ticked/Yes** and **Not Ticked**. By not ticking people were not saying no to any of the headings. What they were saying is that these are not priorities of theirs.

When we look at these responses in terms of importance to those who filled out the survey it turns out like this.

1. **In five years' time I would like to see:**

   - Involvement of youth in the life of the church **77.5%**
   - An active parish pastoral council **67%**
   - Greater involvement of people in parish organisations **67%**
   - Supports for marriage and family life **66%**

- Links with other Christian Churches locally **61.5%**
- Widespread family prayer **56.5%**
- Adult religious education programmes **43.4%**

2. **A vibrant community which:**

- is a caring community **70.8%**
- encourages all vocations **61.3%**
- Is an inclusive community: gender, social status, age etc **61%**
- deepens faith **59.9%**
- hands on faith **54.2%**

When we look at this order of things what does it say to us, if anything? It certainly shows that there is a good mandate from the people for all twelve topics. But there are priorities of importance in that mandate.

There is no surprise in the fact that **involvement of young people** is at the top. Practically every meeting we attended in setting up the twenty-one parish pastoral councils had that as the number one concern.

But it might surprise some people that **61.5%** of people want **closer links with other Christian Churches locally**. This goes against the often accepted view that people don't want Ecumenism.

66% of people want greater **supports for Marriage and family life**. This corresponds well with what people were saying in the previous section about the lack of these supports. It surprises us that at parish and diocesan level those supports are not very strong or proactive. The people surveyed want them to become a priority.

And of course there is a very definite approval for setting up proper parish pastoral councils in every parish: **67%**.

By far the most important quality for our parish communities to develop is that we would be a **Caring Community**: **70.8%**. All the other qualities will flow from there.

This mandate for the future should be listened to very carefully and decisions made accordingly by the parish pastoral councils, the leadership of the parish, and also by the diocesan leadership.

Section 5: A Little about You

Towards the beginning of this chapter we indicated the profile of the respondents to the survey according to gender and age in the twenty-one parishes throughout the Diocese of Derry. Those statistics came from this part of the questionnaire.

Of course there is a lot more to the respondents than those two facts. The most important thing about them is that they represent the ordinary Mass-going people throughout the diocese. They responded very well to being asked to fill in this questionnaire as part of their Eucharist. And they were able to make choices the whole way through.

Not every person answered every question as you can see by the overall numbers recorded at the end of each question. These numbers varied from **17,215** to **10,372** towards the end. This lower number of **10,372** was in response to a question that was applicable to women only.

There can be no doubt that the diocese needs to listen carefully to this very representative body of people, just as each parish that took part in it needs to listen to its own people. Of course other dioceses and other parishes could well find very similar trends for themselves.

1. Are you male/female?
2. Are you a native of the parish?

3. Your age.
4. Do you attend weekday Masses?
5. Do you attend Sunday Masses?
6. Do you feel you belong to this parish?
7. Are you a member of any parish organisation?
8. Are there any issues making it difficult for you to belong?
9. Are you in a relationship not recognised by the Church?
10. There are some parts of the teachings of the Church I am uncomfortable with.
11. As a woman, I feel undervalued.
12. Have experienced hurt in the Church at some time and this has not been healed.

Many important things jump out at us from the responses to these questions.

1. **91.3%** say that they have a feeling of belonging to their parish. That is a wonderful strength to have. It is one that deserves to be nourished.

2. **81.2%** say that they attend Mass every weekend. We can be so conscious of the very many people who no longer go to Mass at all that we easily miss noticing the people who are there week after week. For us as Catholics, Mass is the great sign of faith practice. We need to make sure that it is more and more a celebration of faith and of the faithful. It should not be allowed to simply become a ritual that is without signs of specialness and is performed in the shortest possible time.

3. **Are there any issues making it difficult for you to belong? 10.1%** say **Yes**

Are you in a relationship not recognised by the Church?
5.7% say **Yes**

Are there any parts of the teachings of the Church that you are not comfortable with? 28.3% say **Yes**

As a woman I feel undervalued. 11.7% say **Yes**

I have experienced hurt in the Church at some time and this has not been healed. 7.7% say **Yes**

When we look at these statistics we might feel smug because they are mostly small percentages apart from the **28.3%** who say they are not comfortable with some parts of the teaching of the Church.

These questions however indicate some of the reasons why so many people are no longer with us. It is a great tribute to those who have these experiences and yet remain faithful.

By being more conscious of our people who have these experiences we need to find ways of healing hurt and/or alienation that result from these experiences, beginning with the people who have remained faithful and reaching out to those who have given up on us.

This is an area where diocesan leadership is very important and can be of great help to the people in individual parishes.

4. The question about attendance at weekday Masses is an important one for the parish. **32%** of respondents say that they go to weekday Mass either often or every day. That is a marvellous resource of prayer for the parish.

   It could also become a great resource for building the sense of community in the parish; a source of involving people in service to those in need in the parish; and a source of calling on the gifts of people who easily go unnoticed in the larger community that gathers for weekend Masses.

5. To the question: **Are you a member of any parish organisation** – 18.8% said **Yes**, 79.6% said **No**. This highlights one of the major needs in every parish – how to involve others or at least to help them recognise how they are already involved and how they can become more involved. One of the major tasks of the parish pastoral council is to empower people not just to do things in the parish but to take on responsibility for the growth of the parish as a community of faith.

6. We can take heart from the fact that **71.3%** of those who responded are natives of their parish. This gives a real sense of ownership and this needs to be developed as a real positive.

   The roots of faith are very deep in the lives of the people of the parishes and in the very soil of the parishes through their ancestors. Those roots need to be nurtured and cared for so that they can help bear fruit for the diocese and the world.

The fact that the parish surveys can contribute to building a profile of the local Church in the diocese is not just statistically interesting. It expresses and symbolises the importance of the link between parish and diocese.

Parish pastoral councils are about each individual parish. But no parish is a stand-alone entity. The parish community is intimately related to the diocese as the local Church. It depends on the diocese in many ways; and also contributes to the diocese in many ways.

A New Beginning

The development of parish pastoral councils is the opportunity for a new beginning, not only in the individual parishes but in the relationship of the parishes within the diocese; and the diocese with the parishes. By far the best scenario for parish pastoral councils to begin and to flourish is when they are part of a diocesan project. A parish pastoral council can be very valuable for the individual parish that undertakes to have one. But it is far more valuable when it is part of a diocese that commits itself to this as the way of the present and the future.

However this cannot just be a structural change. It has to be a relationship change. The first significant change in relationships will be noticed at parish level. Where parishioners have seen themselves as passive, or at best as helpers of the priest in the running of the parish, they will begin to participate in leadership with the priest. They will begin to see themselves as partners with the priest, sharing responsibility for the development of the parish. A relationship that was unequal has become collaborative. The process of leadership has become not only collaborative but facilitative, as priest and people enable each other to release the power of the Spirit within each individual and within the faith community.

The relationship change will not just affect the parish. As parish pastoral councils are being established and developed they will enrich the life of the whole diocese. The work of parish pastoral councils and parish pastoral renewal can never be just for the parishes themselves. It will build up the Body of Christ in the whole local Church.

Do Not be Afraid

After sending the crowds away Jesus went up into the hills by himself to pray. When evening came, he was there alone, while the boat, by now far out in the lake, was battling with a heavy sea, for there was a head-wind. In the fourth watch of the night he went towards them, walking on the lake, and when the disciples saw him walking on the lake they were terrified. 'It is a ghost' they said, and cried out in fear. But at once Jesus called out to them saying: 'Courage, it is I. Do not be afraid.' It was Peter who answered: 'Lord', he said, 'if it is you, tell me to come to you across the water.' 'Come', said Jesus. Then Peter got out of the boat and started walking towards Jesus across the water, but as soon as he felt the force of the wind, he took fright and began to sink. 'Lord, save me' he cried. Jesus put out his hand at once and held him. 'Man of little faith', he said, 'why did you doubt?' And as they got into the boat the wind dropped. The people in the boat bowed down before him and said: 'Truly you are the Son of God'. (Mt 14:23–33)

After the Residential Training Weekend

Even though the training weekend was in no way geared to people leaving on a high people generally left it with confidence about the future. They had a good grasp of what a parish pastoral council is about; they had their plans made both long-term and short-term, their structures were in place and the date of their next meeting in their diaries. Everything looked rosy. Nothing could stop them. And thankfully nothing has stopped them. But they began to feel the fear of what they had taken on, and also the self-doubt about whether they were capable. They expressed a need for on-going support.

As we kept in touch with them about how they were progressing – thank God for email as this was such a handy way to keep in touch! – a few different ways in which support was needed emerged and we tried to supply these.

'It is I'

The first and most important way that support is needed is faith in Jesus. Often when people experience a rush of the wonder of faith, as many did in those weekend trainings, they want to save the world. That's a common experience of people who catch a bit of religion. An equally common experience is the harder people work at this the worse things seem to get!

The wonderful thing is we don't have to save the world. In fact we cannot. The task of faithful people is to make it possible for Christ to save the world by holding his hand in one of ours and the hands of our sisters and brothers in the other as we bring them to him. We are the link for them just as so many other people are the links for us.

'Courage! Do not be afraid'

In the scriptures the sentence 'do not be afraid' is by far the most repeated word of God. Fear is identified as the single greatest enemy to faith, to hope and to love.

What Will it Cost Me?

We can have all kinds of fears that hold us back and hinder us in our life of faith. Probably the most significant one is the fear of what it is going to cost us in terms of time, energy and priority. The main commitment of time that a member of a parish pastoral council makes is to a meeting of an hour and a half each month. Without that we certainly can go nowhere. But there has to be an openness to the fact that this meeting will mean spending more time during the month in following up decisions that are being made. That is the part that can scare people and they find themselves holding back. Obviously everyone has to be careful because of other commitments in their lives. But everyone also has to be generous in their commitment to this vital call in their parish. Due to the importance of leadership in the parish pastoral council, people may find that changes need to be made in other aspects of their lives.

Fear of Failure

This is a very common fear that holds so many people back from reaching their true potential. It is a fear that can also hold people back from a full participation in the parish pastoral council. People are forever comparing themselves with others and generally coming off badly because of the comparisons. People can feel inadequate in different ways. It is so very important to overcome this fear in order for each one to bring their unique gifts to the group.

Fear of What other People will Say

One of the spiritual diseases among our Catholic people – it may be there also in other Churches – is criticism of people who generously get involved in order to make the parish stronger. We find this in ordinary, simple, ways like with those who became Ministers of the Word or Ministers of the Eucharist. People are often made to feel self-conscious about their public participation. And others hold back from taking their place in the growth of the community.

This can be a very serious block to people taking on this new leadership role as a member of the parish pastoral council. Every effort needs to be made to eradicate this disease, otherwise the Church cannot move forward. We have to free the laity from thinking of themselves as 'taking over' from the priests or as 'helping' the priests. Lay participation at every level of leadership and of service is both the right and the responsibility of everyone because of our common Baptism. As Catholics we are only learning to live this way of life as the Church. We have a long way to go. And we cannot move in that direction without a lot of support and encouragement.

What are the Sources of this Support?

1. The Parish Community

Within a few weeks of the training weekend for the establishing of the parish pastoral council they are commissioned publicly at one of the Sunday Masses.

This commissioning is meant to mark the truth that they have come from this parish community for the service of the community. None of them are volunteers. They have been selected by the people at the parish assembly and then by that first group including the priest(s). They have generously said yes and the whole community owes them every support.

Sometimes this commissioning is left as a once off occasion. When this happens the parish pastoral council can easily fade into the background and be forgotten. The parish community needs to be reminded regularly of not just the existence of the parish pastoral council but also of the vital importance of it in the present and for the future of the parish.

This ongoing reminder needs to come firstly from the parish pastoral council and how they communicate regularly with the parish community. They can easily fall down on this!

We recommend a monthly newsletter from the parish pastoral council. This could contain an account of the parish pastoral council discussion of that month as well as an agenda for the following month. It should also have input about the developments of the parish pastoral council for the future. And of course encouragement could be given to the parish community to keep growing as a faith community.

The parish pastoral council should also produce an annual report of where they have come from, where they are now, and where they hope to go in the year ahead. This report could be presented at an annual parish assembly.

The priest(s), as part of the parish pastoral council also has a key role to play in reminding the parish community of the importance of the parish pastoral council.

2. Diocesan Leadership

Support for parish pastoral councils needs to be seen to be coming from the diocesan leadership. Otherwise it can easily deteriorate into being seen as the whim of individual priests and a few people.

The parish pastoral council is talked about as a new form of leadership in the parish. It is specifically leadership in developing the pastoral care and the pastoral potential of all the people of the parish.

It is a new form of leadership because it involves partnership of parishioners with the priest(s) and with one another to discern the needs and the potentials, to decide the priorities, to implement these decisions and to constantly involve others as leaders in implementation.

This all needs to be reflected in how the diocesan leadership communicates with the parish. Otherwise nothing much changes. Diocesan communication with the parish needs to be progressively seen as communication with the parish pastoral council. This gives them their place of leadership. It also acknowledges the priest as part of this shared leadership. It is an important change that highlights the reality of a new form of leadership.

The parish pastoral council also needs the support of the diocesan leadership through occasions like an annual retreat for all the parish pastoral councils; an annual review with all the parish pastoral councils gathered with the diocesan leadership; an occasional note of encouragement from the diocesan leadership to the parishes to keep the parish pastoral council to the forefront until it becomes an integral part of what it means to be a parish.

3. **Doing it on Purpose**

As well as needing the external support from the parish community and from the diocesan authorities, the members of the parish pastoral council need to develop their own inner strength and a positive attitude to what they have taken on. Again, that begins with faith:

> May the God of our Lord Jesus Christ, the Father of glory, give you a spirit of wisdom and perception of what is revealed, to bring you to full knowledge of him. May he enlighten the eyes of your mind so that you can see what hope his call holds for

you, what rich glories he has promised the saints will inherit and how infinitely great is the power that he has exercised for us believers. This you can tell from the strength of his power at work in Christ, when he used it to raise him from the dead and to make him sit at his right hand, in heaven, far above every sovereignty, authority, power, or domination, or any other name that can be named, not only in this age but also in the age to come. He has put all things under his feet, and made him, as ruler of everything, the head of the Church; which is his body, the fullness of him who fills the whole creation. (Eph 1:17–21)

But it also involves a conscious effort to mobilise the personal gifts that each person has, and to refuse to be held back by fears and negativity.

The fear that we are dealing with is not necessarily a traumatic fear. It is not that we feel threatened in ourselves. The fear that we are dealing with is a low level inhibiting fear, a fear that makes us hesitant. The result of it is that we don't act decisively, that we settle into a routine expecting someone else to take the initiative, to tell us what to do.

We should not be surprised at this fear and inhibition. After all, we are entering into a new experience of leadership, after generations of a culture of diffidence and perhaps even subservience. Not only the laity, but also the clergy – especially the clergy – have grown up in an atmosphere of wariness and caution about straying across the boundaries of their appropriate roles. That wariness has been known to lead to a syndrome called 'learned helplessness', which means that if I suspect there may be a negative reaction to my behaviour, I tailor my behaviour to the level of least risk. In other words, I self-censor my behaviour well within the boundaries of any possible annoyance.

The one thing we need to avoid is wasting time and energy in complaining about the past. But we do need to put a lot of effort into re-directing our energies for the future. Instead of waiting for someone else to tell us what to do, we need to confront our fears and inhibitions, and build up our internal resources of positive expectation, reassurance and conscious decision-making. This will be supported particularly by sharing faith and vision within the parish pastoral council, in a process of prayerful discernment. The parish pastoral council will be able to lead the parish, by word and example, into being a conscious Catholic faith community, an intentional Catholic parish.

Archbishop Eamon Martin of Armagh in *Intercom* (July/August 2016), wrote about the essence of an intentional Catholic family:

> Essentially for me, an 'intentional Catholic family' is one where parents and children are clear about the difference that their faith can and does make to their everyday life.
>
> This is what we do because we are a Catholic family! Our faith is obvious in our daily routines. We go to Mass on Sundays and holy days; we pray together; we do not waste; we say the Rosary; we protect our family as much as we can from the evil influences of alcohol, drugs and internet addiction; we do our best to give good example; we have religious symbols prominently on display in our homes; we do penance of some kind every Friday; we go to Confession together; we fast for Lent and we abstain on Ash Wednesday and Good Friday; we visit and look after the sick and elderly members of our extended family; we bear wrongs patiently and forgive one another when family quarrels begin; we do not tolerate violence or abuse of any kind in our home; we visit our family graves and we pray for our dead …

Many of the marks of the intentional Catholic family, as identified by Archbishop Martin, can apply also to the Catholic parish, and certainly the whole idea of a Catholic parish 'doing it on purpose' – being an intentional Catholic parish – is a vision that should motivate a parish pastoral council.

4. Strategies for Engagement

Another aspect of personal reassurance and positive leadership is to acknowledge our conscious and subconscious strategies for taking on serious responsibility in the parish, or conversely for avoiding the full implications of being part of a genuine collaborative leadership.

A very important indication of a parish pastoral council's strategy of engagement in the work of responsible leadership is the commitment of members to a conscious partnership approach.

A New Way of Being Church

Building partnership between priest and people is a whole new way of being Church – or is it? It certainly is not the way that we have been used to. But there are indications of it in the early Church of the Acts of the Apostles, the Letters of Paul, Peter, John etc., and the vision of the Book of Revelation.

How can we work on this today? The following is a list of the qualities of partners. This list has come from priests and people as we worked with them on training weekends and other workshops. We also include a list of what promotes partnership. Again all of these come from people's life experience.

What are the qualities of partners?	
Trust	Openness
Loyalty	Respect
Supportive	Able to negotiate
Able to communicate	Honesty
Risk-taker	Enthusiastic
Faith	Common goal
Tolerance	Sensitivity
Concern for the other	Fairness
Good listener	Determination
Flexibility	Sense of humour
Positivity	Willingness to compromise
Willingness to learn	Patience
Courage	Resilience
Self-awareness	Team player
Willing to co-operate	Action, not just talk
Able to delegate	Reliability
Vision	Equality
Accepting different roles	Accepting different skills
Confidentiality	Cater for individual needs/ages
Ability to debate	

What promotes partnership?	
Value everyone's view	Inclusiveness
Communication out from PC	Decisions through consensus
Welcoming others as partners	Listen to others beyond the group
Guided by the Holy Spirit	Importance of fun

Clear objectives – confidence	Belief in where we are going
Open/honest	What each one has to say valued
Feeling of being needed	Work as a team

What blocks partnership?	
Lack of vision	Poor communication
Lack of leadership	Lack of common goals
Ignoring other's opinions	Being watery
Cliques real or perceived	Lack of confidence
Lack of openness	Setting limits on ourselves
Fear – cannot do that!	Setting limits on others

It can be a useful exercise to go through these lists at meetings of the parish pastoral council taking the items one by one, and examining how each one applies to your group just now, and what you can do together to develop each one, to keep building a partnership approach.

Another strategy of engagement is to work on developing prayer as a more influential part of your meeting. Dedicate ten minutes to prayer sometime during the course of the meeting. Each one should be included leading this. That can scare a lot of people but it can be done with good preparation and with each one taking initiative.

Every effort to develop the parish pastoral council, to run the meetings effectively and to see that they are followed up seriously, will lead to real engagement in leadership and real pastoral development. This will include:

1. Continually refreshing the agenda for the meetings of the pastoral council, looking again at the priorities which were identified in the survey questionnaire and the parish assembly and finding ways to listen to the parish community and to involve them.

2. regularly surfacing names of people who could be asked to get involved. It's important to keep building up this list, believing in the goodness of people you know in your family and among your friends and neighbours. Look at the people who go to Mass at the weekend. Look at those who go to Mass during the week. Name all of them for yourselves. These are your riches.

1. Strategies for Avoidance

It is most important to keep building on the positive strategies of engagement, taking note of what leads to good leadership and the development of a vibrant parish. But it can also help to keep an eye out for things that can slow us down, for the conscious or unconscious strategies of avoidance. Among those are:

a. A vagueness or lack of clarity about what a parish pastoral council is, expressed by calling it a parish council, or 'our committee'. If we settle for 'parish council' we can change the focus so easily to administration (and sometimes people are more at ease with this). If we call ourselves a committee we lose the dynamic of discerning, deciding, implementing and involving others (and sometimes people are more at ease with this also). The name parish pastoral council keeps the focus on the people of the parish, their needs and their potentials and also their call to be 'a royal priesthood, a holy nation, a people set apart to proclaim the glory of the Lord'.

b. Misunderstanding, fear, or hesitation about individual roles. Among the lay members this can take the form of self-deprecation: 'we're not good enough, or knowledgeable enough, or smart enough'. Among the priests it can take the form of perceiving the parish pastoral council as a threat to their position and power (clericalism is not quite extinct), or the mentality that the status quo 'will do me my day'. Among both priests and laity it is still possible to come across those who hanker for 'the good old days', as if they wanted to go back to some former type of Church. We have a great responsibility to move forward, drawn by the Holy Spirit and the adventure of the Gospel of joy.

c. The ordinary human pitfalls like power-struggles, personality clashes, or other disagreements. It is so important that people sort these out quickly through prayer and sharing. But where these come from the fact that one person is a priest or another is a lay person there has been a serious breakdown in the processes that are essential for living as a faith community.

d. Seeing the parish pastoral council as just one of many good and important things to promote and develop in the diocese. It then becomes a matter for individual taste and inclination whether any initiative is taken. There is no appreciation of the unique value of the parish pastoral council as a pivotal structure in the local Church which will give a different flavour to everything else – the flavour of a shared partnership leadership between priests and parishioners. When the key role of the pastoral council is acknowledged, that will be reflected in the commitment of time, energy and priority.

e. Strategies of avoidance that are experienced in the context of the meetings of the parish pastoral council. These may be subconscious, perhaps little more than slothfulness or lack of attention, but the effects can be just as harmful. One example is where the agenda has not been properly set up. Time is wasted and sometimes very little gets done.

Another example is where people just chat rather than engage in fruitful discussion or sharing. Groups of all kinds get into bad habits of this and it can be very difficult to pull it back from there without offending some. Keeping the discipline of a meeting is very important for the well-being of a group.

A third example is where people come to a meeting without preparing for it, or neglecting to bring all relevant documentation. For a parish pastoral council to work properly it is vital that every member takes full responsibility for what happens at the meetings and that what has been decided will happen after the meeting. A group that carelessly leaves the running of meetings only to the chairperson or secretary is doomed to fail.

The Gift of Persistence

None of these tendencies of human nature should cause us to despair. Strategies of avoidance or fears or hesitations should just give us fresh motivation. One gift we need in the Christian life and in the pastoral life is the gift of persistence, or perhaps we should say the gift of boldness. The disciples in chapter four of the Acts of the Apostles prayed: 'Lord, help your servants to proclaim your message with all boldness' (Acts 4:29).

The Church is on an exciting, even if, at times, a dangerous journey in the world today. We need a lot of good, positive leadership to keep us professing, not just in words, but in how we live our lives, the extraordinary faith that we are gifted with.

At the end of the Gospel passage which was quoted at the beginning of this chapter we hear that when Jesus and Peter got back into the boat the sea was suddenly calm. And the disciples at last recognised and acknowledged Jesus as the Christ.

We have to work hard to develop appropriate structures at parish and diocesan level. But we work with confidence, knowing that Jesus is with us always, and that we are led by the Spirit. We are not working for the sake of the structures, but for the sake of the Gospel. It is all about evangelisation.

In 1975, marking ten years from the close of the Second Vatican Council, Pope Paul VI wrote the wonderful document *Evangelii Nuntiandi*. It hasn't lost any of its power in the intervening years. Pope Paul VI writes of an evangelised and evangelising Church:

> The Church is an evangeliser, but she begins by being evangelised herself. She is the People of God immersed in the world, and often tempted by idols, and she always needs to hear the proclamation of 'the mighty works of God' which converted her to the Lord; she always needs to be called together afresh by him and reunited. In brief, this means that she has a constant need of being evangelised, if she wishes to retain freshness, vigour and strength in order to proclaim the Gospel. The Second Vatican Council recalled, and the 1974 Synod vigorously took up again this theme of the Church which is evangelised by constant conversion and renewal, in order to evangelise the world with credibility.'
> (*Evangelii Nuntiandi*, 15)

Leon-Joseph Cardinal Suenens of Belgium played a significant part in the Second Vatican Council in the nineteen sixties. As he looked ahead to the end of the twentieth century, he wrote this beautiful 'Prayer for the Year 2000'. It includes the phrase, 'on the eve of the Third Millennium'. We are no longer on the eve of the Third Millennium but this prayer is just as relevant today, perhaps more relevant, in the world in which we live:

Looking at the World ...

> Lord, we are afraid to face the world of tomorrow;
> we have lost faith in ourselves;
> we no longer believe in that boundless progress
> which was supposed to ensure our future happiness;
> nor do we believe any longer in science as the salvation of
> the world;
> nor do we believe that we humans are our own supreme
> end;
> nor that death is the last word of life.

> And we know, too, that if tomorrow there were to be
> another nuclear disaster such as Chernobyl,
> whether by accident or design,
> there could be an apocalyptic explosion
> from which none of us would survive,
> no-one even to number and bury the dead.

Looking at the Church ...

> Lord, if I turn my eyes to the Church,
> who received from your Son the promise of eternal life,
> I feel how poor and weak we, your disciples, are today;
> so poor and so poorly Christian;
> but I hear on every side

the pressing call of our pastors
for a new and second evangelisation
to make us true and faithful Christians,
conscious of the imperatives of our Baptism.

Help us to discover the fervour of the early Christians
and the power of the first evangelisation,
that morning of Pentecost, as it started in the Cenacle of Jerusalem
where your disciples with Mary, gathered in prayer,
awaited, Father, the fulfilment of your promise.

Give us the grace to be renewed
'in the Spirit and in fire'.
Teach us to speak to the world in tongues of fire.
Let us bring to an end this time of uncertainty
where Christians are timid and mute,
discussing anxiously problems of today,
as in the past on the road from Jerusalem to Emmaus,
without realising that the Master is risen and alive.

Prayer for the Future ...

Lord, open our hearts to welcome your Holy Spirit;
teach us to await his coming,
as Mary did, at the time of the Annunciation
and again at Pentecost – the Nativity of the Church –
when she became also our Mother.
Teach the coming generations that your Son, Jesus Christ,
remains for ever and ever, the Saviour of the world.

Help us to proclaim, loudly and boldly, that he is
'the Way,

the Truth
and the Life'.

The Way, which leads us towards our final destiny.
The Truth, which lights our way through the night.
The Life, which gives us a profound peace, serenity and joy
which nothing created can destroy.

May your disciples, on the eve of the Third Millennium,
hasten their steps to obey the order given by the Master,
to be 'One' in the unity of
the Father,
the Son,
the Holy Spirit,
and may they approach the Lord together,
radiant with his light,
with no shadow on their face,
so that the whole world will recognise Jesus Christ
alive in his disciples,
now and for ever.
Amen.

Questionnaire Responses

Relationships and Involvement in the Parish

The quality of relationships between priest(s) and people is

Parish	Very good	Good	Fair	Poor	Don't know	Questionnaires Completed
Average in per cent	46.9	36.6	10.56	3.0	2.8	17,213

Relationships between the people and the schools are

Parish	Very good	Good	Fair	Poor	Don't know	Questionnaires Completed
Average in per cent	26.2	41.2	12.6	2.5	17.3	17,097

The work of parish organisations is

Parish	Very good	Good	Fair	Poor	Don't know	Questionnaires Completed
Average in per cent	26.0	42.0	12.6	2.5	11.90	15,820

Co-operation between parish organisations is

Parish	Very good	Good	Fair	Poor	Don't know	Questionnaires Completed
Average in per cent	15.7	33.1	13.5	3.1	20.7	13,646

Involvement of women in the parish is

Parish	Very good	Good	Fair	Poor	Don't know	Questionnaires Completed
Average in per cent	24.4	44.6	16.3	4.1	10.3	16,579

Involvement of men in the parish is

Parish	Very good	Good	Fair	Poor	Don't know	Questionnaires Completed
Average in per cent	20.2	46.7	19.1	4.6	9.2	16,532

The process of decision making in the parish is

Parish	Very good	Good	Fair	Poor	Don't know	Questionnaires Completed
Average in per cent	12.5	33.7	20.3	9.2	23.6	15,766

Involvement of youth in the parish is

Parish	Very good	Good	Fair	Poor	Don't know	Questionnaires Completed
Average in per cent	12.3	28.1	26.7	19.1	13.2	16,417

The level and range of parish based social activities is

Parish	Very good	Good	Fair	Poor	Don't know	Questionnaires Completed
Average in per cent	8.2	27.5	27.7	22.8	13.2	16,430

Relationships with other Christian Churches locally

Parish	Very good	Good	Fair	Poor	Don't know	Questionnaires Completed
Average in per cent	12.1	36.8	19.9	9.4	21.5	16,570

Support for families in the parish is

Parish	Very good	Good	Fair	Poor	Don't know	Questionnaires Completed
Average in per cent	20.8	39.6	17.8	5.7	15.6	15,234

Support for bereaved people is

Parish	Very good	Good	Fair	Poor	Don't know	Questionnaires Completed
Average in per cent	31.1	34.9	11.7	5.2	16.7	16,513

Support for elderly people is

Parish	Very good	Good	Fair	Poor	Don't know	Questionnaires Completed
Average in per cent	26.6	37.8	14.0	5.2	15.8	16,554

Support for people with disabilities is

Parish	Very good	Good	Fair	Poor	Don't know	Questionnaires Completed
Average in per cent	18.0	31.8	15.7	6.9	27.1	16,433

Support for sick people is

Parish	Very good	Good	Fair	Poor	Don't know	Questionnaires Completed
Average in per cent	32.5	39.2	10.9	3.4	13.5	16,554

Support for marriages in difficulties is

Parish	Very good	Good	Fair	Poor	Don't know	Questionnaires Completed
Average in per cent	7.3	19.0	13.8	8.3	51.2	16,499

Support for teenagers and young people is

Parish	Very good	Good	Fair	Poor	Don't know	Questionnaires Completed
Average in per cent	8.1	24.3	21.8	14.9	30.3	16,496

Support for single adults in the parish is

Parish	Very good	Good	Fair	Poor	Don't know	Questionnaires Completed
Average in per cent	5.7	21.4	18.7	10.1	43.4	16,447

Relationships among parishioners are

Parish	Very good	Good	Fair	Poor	Don't know	Questionnaires Completed
Average in per cent	17.8	49.1	18.0	3.7	10.9	16,523

Sacraments in the Parish

Baptism arrangements and support

Parish	No change Needed	Could be Improved	Must be Changed	Unable to Comment	Questionnaires Completed
Average in per cent	57.5	9.7	1.0	30.9	16,948

First Holy Communion arrangements

Parish	No change Needed	Could be Improved	Must be Changed	Unable to Comment	Questionnaires Completed
Average in per cent	64.5	7.2	1.5	26.3	16,998

Arrangements for Confirmation

Parish	No change Needed	Could be Improved	Must be Changed	Unable to Comment	Questionnaires Completed
Average in per cent	61.0	8.3	2.2	28.2	16,916

Support for Marriage preparation

Parish	No change Needed	Could be Improved	Must be Changed	Unable to Comment	Questionnaires Completed
Average in per cent	44.2	12.2	1.8	41.2	16,923

Arrangements for Marriage

Parish	No change Needed	Could be Improved	Must be Changed	Unable to Comment	Questionnaires Completed
Average in per cent	45.9	10.1	1.3	42.1	16,285

Support for couples after Marriage

Parish	No change Needed	Could be Improved	Must be Changed	Unable to Comment	Questionnaires Completed
Average in per cent	30.2	21.2	2.5	45.5	16,865

Arrangements for funerals

Parish	No change Needed	Could be Improved	Must be Changed	Unable to Comment	Questionnaires Completed
Average in per cent	68.2	7.1	1.0	23.0	16,960

Arrangements for Sacrament of the Sick

Parish	No change Needed	Could be Improved	Must be Changed	Unable to Comment	Questionnaires Completed
Average in per cent	61.0	8.0	1.0	30.0	16,904

Times of weekend Masses

Parish	No change Needed	Could be Improved	Must be Changed	Unable to Comment	Questionnaires Completed
Average in per cent	71.2	15.1	4.7	3.7	16,461

Participation by lay people in Masses

Parish	No change Needed	Could be Improved	Must be Changed	Unable to Comment	Questionnaires Completed
Average in per cent	62.4	22.3	2.7	11.9	16,885

Parish Resources

Involvement of Laity essential part of Parish Life

Parish	Yes	No	Unable to comment	Questionnaires Completed
Average in per cent	79.6	4.7	14.9	16,831

Prepared to become more involved in work of the parish

Parish	Yes	No	Unable to comment	Questionnaires Completed
Average in per cent	49.0	33.4	17.6	16,793

Am well informed about parish activities, events and news

Parish	Yes	No	Unable to comment	Questionnaires Completed
Average in per cent	71.2	19.6	8.3	16,848

Find the weekly bulletin helpful

Parish	Yes	No	Unable to comment	Questionnaires Completed
Average in per cent	88.5	3.2	4.4	16,261

I contribute regularly to Church Collections

Parish	Yes	No	Unable to comment	Questionnaires Completed
Average in per cent	87.0	8.2	4.4	17,002

I am eligible for and have entered the Gift Aid/Covenant scheme

Parish	Yes	No	Unable to comment	Questionnaires Completed
Average in per cent	34.5	42.0	23.2	16,788

I understand and know where my Contributions are being used

Parish	Yes	No	Unable to comment	Questionnaires Completed
Average in per cent	53.0	32.6	13.5	16,821

The Parish In The Future –
By the year … I would like to see

An active parish pastoral council

Parish	Ticked/Yes	Not ticked	Questionnaires Completed
Average in per cent	67.0	33.0	14,124

Adult Religious Education programmes

Parish	Ticked/Yes	Not ticked	Questionnaires Completed
Average in per cent	43.4	56.6	12,281

Supports for Marriage & family life

Parish	Ticked/Yes	Not ticked	Questionnaires Completed
Average in per cent	66.0	34.0	13,969

Widespread family prayer

Parish	Ticked/Yes	Not ticked	Questionnaires Completed
Average in per cent	56.5	43.5	13,746

Involvement of youth in the life of the Church

Parish	Ticked/Yes	Not ticked	Questionnaires Completed
Average in per cent	77.5	22.5	14,579

Links with other Christian Churches locally

Parish	Ticked/Yes	Not ticked	Questionnaires Completed
Average in per cent	61.5	38.5	13,641

Greater involvement of people in parish organisations

Parish	Ticked/Yes	Not ticked	Questionnaires Completed
Average in per cent	67.0	33.0	14,158

I would like to see a vibrant community which: deepens faith

Parish	Ticked/Yes	Not ticked	Questionnaires Completed
Average in per cent	59.9	40.1	14,066

I would like to see a vibrant community which: hands on the faith

Parish	Ticked/Yes	Not ticked	Questionnaires Completed
Average in per cent	54.2	45.8	13,801

I would like to see a vibrant community which: encourages all vocations

Parish	Ticked/Yes	Not ticked	Questionnaires Completed
Average in per cent	61.3	38.7	14,337

I would like to see a vibrant community which: is an inclusive community (gender, social status, age, etc)

Parish	Ticked/Yes	Not ticked	Questionnaires Completed
Average in per cent	61.00	39.0	14,071

I would like to see a vibrant community which: Is a caring community

Parish	Ticked/Yes	Not ticked	Questionnaires Completed
Average in per cent	70.8	29.2	14,674

A Little about You

Are you male/female?

Parish	Male	Female	Questionnaires Completed
Average in per cent	39.7	58.6	14,746

Are you a native of the parish?

Parish	Male	Female	Questionnaires Completed
Average in per cent	71.3	27.3	13,879

Your age

Parish	12-18	19-30	31-55	56-70	Over 70	Questionnaires Completed
Average in per cent	11.8	10.5	39.7	25.0	11.1	14,800

Do you attend weekday Masses?

Parish	Never	Seldom	Often	Every day	Questionnaires Completed
Average in per cent	20.3	44.8	22.8	9.2	14,577

Do you attend Sunday Masses?

Parish	Seldom	Often	Every week	Questionnaires Completed
Average in per cent	3.4	13.7	81.2	14,979

Do you feel you belong to this parish?

Parish	Yes	No	Questionnaires Completed
Average in per cent	91.3	7.2	16,315

Are you a member of any parish organisation?

Parish	Yes	No	Questionnaires Completed
Average in per cent	18.8	79.6	16,207

Are there any issues making it difficult for you to belong?

Parish	Yes	No	Questionnaires Completed
Average in per cent	10.1	87.4	14,714

Are you in a relationship not recognised by the Church?

Parish	Yes	No	Questionnaires Completed
Average in per cent	5.7	90.5	13,707

There are some parts of the teachings of the Church I am uncomfortable with

Parish	Yes	No	Questionnaires Completed
Average in per cent	28.3	68.0	14,486

As a woman, I feel undervalued

Parish	Yes	No	(Men) Not applicable	Questionnaires Completed
Average in per cent	11.7	70.9		10,372

Have experienced hurt in the Church at some time and this has not been healed

Parish	Yes	No	Questionnaires completed
Average in per cent	7.7	87.9	13,210

Bibliography

1. *Vatican Council II, Constitutions, Decrees, Declarations*, Austin Flannery OP, Dominican Publications, 1996.

2. *Vatican II By Those Who Were There*, Alberic Stacpoole, Geoffrey Chapman, 1986.

3. *The Code of Canon Law*, Collins, 1983.

4. *The Catechism of the Catholic Church*, Veritas, 1994.

5. *Irish Catholic Catechism for Adults*, Veritas, 2014.

6. *General Directory for Catechesis*, Congregation for the Clergy, Veritas, 1998.

7. 'Share the Good News', *National Directory for Catechesis in Ireland*, Irish Episcopal Conference, Veritas, 2010.

8. 'The Vocation and Mission of the Laity' (*Christifideles Laici*), Pope John Paul II, Veritas, 1989.

9. 'At the Beginning of the New Millennium' (*Novo Millennio Ineunte*), Pope John Paul II, Veritas 2001.

10. *Church Membership and Pastoral Co-responsibility*, Pope Benedict XVI. Address at the opening of the Pastoral Convention of the Diocese of Rome, Basilica of Saint John Lateran, May 2009.

11. 'The Joy of the Gospel' (*Evangelii Gaudium*), Pope Francis, Veritas, 2013.

12. 'On Care for our Common Home' (*Laudato Si*), Pope Francis, Veritas, 2015.

13. 'The Joy of Love' (*Amoris Laetitia*), Pope Francis, Veritas, 2016.

14. 'Parish Pastoral Councils', *A Framework for Developing Diocesan Norms and Parish Guidelines*, Irish Episcopal Conference, Veritas, 2007.

15. *Living Communion*, Irish Episcopal Conference, Veritas, 2012.

16. *Partnership in Parish*, Enda Lyons, Columba Press, 1987.

17. 'Think Big, Act Small', *Working at Collaborative Ministry through Parish Pastoral Councils*, Johnny Doherty CSsR, Oliver Crilly, Frank Dolaghan, Paddi Curran, Veritas, 2005.

18. *A Handbook for Parish Councils*, Jane Ferguson (Dublin Diocesan Guidelines), Columba Press, 2005.

19. 'Parish Pastoral Councils', *A Formation Manual*, Debra Snoddy, Jim Campbell and Andrew McNally, Veritas, 2010.

20. 'Pastoral Councils', *Making Communion Visible*, Breandán Leahy, Doctrine and Life, April 2005.

21. 'Ministry Now', *New Approaches for a Changing Church*, Martin Kennedy, Veritas, 2006.

22. 'Tomorrow's Parish', *A Vision and a Path*, Donal Harrington, Columba Press, 2015.

23. *Making Good Decisions*, Brian Grogan S.J., Veritas, 2015.

Other Resources

'ASK', *A movement of Continuous Prayer for Marriage and Family Life*, Fr Johnny Doherty, C.Ss.R.

www.continuousprayer.net